The
Inquisition

Titles in the World History Series

WORLD HISTORY SERIES ■ ■ ■

The Inquisition

by
Deborah Bachrach

Lucent Books, P.O. Box 289011, San Diego, CA 92198-9011

For Clio and all the others

Library of Congress Cataloging-in-Publication Data

Bachrach, Deborah, 1943-
   The inquisition / by Deborah Bachrach.
      p. cm.—(World history series)
   Includes bibliographical references and index.
   ISBN 1-56006-247-9 (alk. paper)
   1. Inquisition—Juvenile literature. [1. Inquisition.]
 I. Title. II. Series.
BX1712.B33   1995
272'.2—dc20   94-11567
                                             CIP
                                            AC

Contents

Foreword

Each year on the first day of school, nearly every history teacher faces the task of explaining why his or her students should study history. One logical answer to this question is that exploring what happened in our past explains how the things we often take for granted—our customs, ideas, and institutions—came to be. As statesman and historian Winston Churchill put it, "Every nation or group of nations has its own tale to tell. Knowledge of the trials and struggles is necessary to all who would comprehend the problems, perils, challenges, and opportunities which confront us today." Thus, a study of history puts modern ideas and institutions in perspective. For example, though the founders of the United States were talented and creative thinkers, they clearly did not invent the concept of democracy. Instead, they adapted some democratic ideas that had originated in ancient Greece and with which the Romans, the British, and others had experimented. An exploration of these cultures, then, reveals their very real connection to us through institutions that continue to shape our daily lives.

Another reason often given for studying history is the idea that lessons exist in the past from which contemporary societies can benefit and learn. This idea, although controversial, has always been an intriguing one for historians. Those who agree that society can benefit from the past often quote philosopher George Santayana's famous statement, "Those who cannot remember the past are condemned to repeat it." Historians who ascribe to Santayana's philosophy believe that, for example, studying the events that led up to the major world wars or other significant historical events would allow society to chart a different and more favorable course in the future.

Just as difficult as convincing students to realize the importance of studying history is the search for useful and interesting supplementary materials that present historical events in a context that can be easily understood. The volumes in Lucent Books' World History Series attempt to present a broad, balanced, and penetrating view of the march of history. Ancient Egypt's important wars and rulers, for example, are presented against the rich and colorful backdrop of Egyptian religious, social, and cultural developments. The series engages the reader by enhancing historical events with these cultural contexts. For example, in *Ancient Greece*, the text covers the role of women in that society. Slavery is discussed in *The Roman Empire*, as well as how slaves earned their freedom. The numerous and varied aspects of everyday life in these and other societies are explored in each volume of the series. Additionally, the series covers the major political, cultural, and philosophical ideas as the torch of civilization is passed from ancient Mesopotamia and Egypt, through Greece, Rome, Medieval Europe, and other world cultures, to the modern day.

The material in the series is formatted in a thorough, precise, and organized manner. Each volume offers the reader a comprehensive and clearly written overview of an important historical event or period. The topic under discussion is placed in a broad, historical context. For example, *The Italian Renaissance* begins with a discussion of the High Middle Ages and the loss of central control that allowed certain Italian cities to develop artistically. The book ends by looking forward to the Reformation and interpreting the societal changes that grew out of the Renaissance. Thus, students are not only involved in an historical era, but also enveloped by the events leading up to that era and the events following it.

One important and unique feature in the World History Series is the primary and secondary source quotations that richly supplement each volume. These quotes are useful in a number of ways. First, they allow students access to sources they would not normally be exposed to because of the difficulty and obscurity of the original source. The quotations range from interesting anecdotes to far-sighted cultural perspectives and are drawn from historical witnesses both past and present. Second, the quotes demonstrate how and where historians themselves derive their information on the past as they strive to reach a consensus on historical events. Lastly, all of the quotes are footnoted, familiarizing students with the citation process and allowing them to verify quotes and/or look up the original source if the quote piques their interest.

Finally, the books in the World History Series provide a detailed launching point for further research. Each book contains a bibliography specifically geared toward student research. A second, annotated bibliography introduces students to all the sources the author consulted when compiling the book. A chronology of important dates gives students an overview, at a glance, of the topic covered. Where applicable, a glossary of terms is included.

In short, the series is designed not only to acquaint readers with the basics of history, but also to make them aware that their lives are a part of an ongoing human saga. Perhaps they will then come to the same realization as famed historian Arnold Toynbee. In his monumental work, *A Study of History,* he wrote about becoming aware of history flowing through him in a mighty current, and of his own life "welling like a wave in the flow of this vast tide."

Important Dates in the History of the Inquisition

1184	1200	1250	1300	1350	1400	1450	1500	155

1184
Pope Lucius III orders all bishops to make inquiries into the subject of heresy

1208
Pope Innocent III's representative is assassinated in the Languedoc region of France

1209
Innocent III begins the Albigensian crusade against the Cathars in Languedoc

1215
Fourth Lateran Council announces laws of the church governing the treatment of heresy

1233
Pope Gregory IX orders Dominicans to go to Languedoc, marking the official beginning of the Inquisition in Languedoc

1252
Pope Innocent IV issues *Ad extirpanda*, the papal bull giving the Inquisition great powers, including the power to torture suspected heretics

1256
Pope Alexander IV empowers inquisitors to absolve one another from having acted harshly in obtaining confessions

1290
Jews expelled from England

1307
Campaign in France against the Knights Templar begins, ending in the destruction of the famous crusading order

1309
Jews expelled from France

1360
Publication of the *Directorium inquisitorum* of Nicholas Eymerich

1391
Pogroms in Spain

1415
Jan Hus burned at the stake

1430
Joan of Arc captured by the English

1431
Joan of Arc burned at the stake in Rouen

1474
Inquisition established in Aragon

1478
Isabella of Spain instructs representatives in papal court to apply to Pope Sixtus IV for papal bull that would give her power to establish the Inquisition in Castille

1478-1483
The Inquisition gradually established throughout the rest of Spain

1482
King Ferdinand establishes the Inquisition in Aragon

1484
Pope Innocent VIII issues the Witch Bull

1486
Publication of Henry Kramer and Jakob Sprenger's *Malleus maleficarum,* or *The Hammer of Witches*

1490
La Guardia trials begin early in year and culminate in a series of convictions and executions in November 1491

1492
Jews expelled from Spain

1498
Trial and burning of Girolamo Savonarola

1545
Council of Trent: Catholic Church condemns Protestantism

1559
Papal Index is established in Rome

1571
Congregation of the Index created by Pope Pius V

1580-1640
Spain takes over Portugal and establishes the Inquisition there

1600
Trial and burning of Giordano Bruno

1632
Galileo is tried by the Inquisition for the first time

1789
Outbreak of French Revolution leads to attacks on the church and on the Inquisition

1852
Inquisition is abolished in Rome

1948
Last official list of condemned books is published

1966
Index is suspended

1992
King Juan Carlos of Spain invites Jews to return to their ancestral homeland

1993
Roman Catholic Church states that it is possible to reconcile views of Galileo with those of the church

What Was the Inquisition?

"The Inquisition" was not a single entity. It was not an investigation, a court, or a torture chamber, although it often had all these components. Rather, the Inquisition was a series of many-armed tribunals through which the Catholic Church attempted to achieve and maintain uniformity of religious thought and practice. To this end, the church empowered its own officials, called inquisitors, to find people who might be guilty of beliefs or actions contrary to church teachings.

Men and women so accused were subjected to coercion to induce them to confess. Sometimes the coercion was psychological; in many cases it was intensely physical. Some survived and were released; others were imprisoned or turned over to civil authorities to be executed.

The Power of the Papacy

"The Inquisition" consisted of the powerful clergymen and their agents who administered and manned the system of investigations, courts, and prisons that came to be known as the Holy Office. Inquisitions began in France in the thirteenth century and had spread throughout

Once convicted of heresy by the inquisitorial court, many prisoners were executed. Here, condemned heretics are escorted to the town plaza, where they will be burned at the stake.

A medieval drawing depicts the celebration of a Catholic mass. As the most important institution in Western Europe, the Catholic Church exerted tremendous power over the political and spiritual life of the people.

Europe by the late Middle Ages. The centuries-long Spanish Inquisition was the most notorious, although other inquisitions flourished for shorter periods.

From the fifteenth century on, European monarchs took advantage of the machinery of the Inquisition to rid themselves of opponents like Joan of Arc, whom they could not neutralize through war or diplomacy. Throughout its history, however, the Inquisition was the creature of the Catholic Church. The church began to fragment in the mid-1500s, but the Holy Office remained under the authority of the pope in Rome.

At the end of the twelfth century the Catholic Church, led by the pope, who resided in Rome, was the most important institution in Europe. It was in many ways the heir of the Roman Empire. "Catholic" comes from the Greek word meaning "universal," and indeed, almost all people born in Europe were members of the Catholic Church. Under a series of powerful popes, culminating in the pontificate of Innocent III, the church came close to establishing a papal monarchy that controlled the political as well as the spiritual life of Western Europe.

In a medieval village, the church building was the most important structure. The population did not stray far from the sound of the church bells, and almost all activities were conducted within the church itself. People were baptized in the church, received its sacraments throughout life, and then were buried in consecrated ground.

Legal matters, and particularly wills, involving the settlement of landholdings were also arranged through the church. Most educational opportunities were provided through the church, since as a rule the clergy were virtually the only people who could read and write.

But at the moment of its greatest authority, the power of the church was threatened. In some parts of Europe, Catholics began to stray from traditional religious teachings. Ordinary people condemned the wealth and worldliness of many members of the church hierarchy—bishops and cardinals, for example. At the same time, they were alarmed by the lack of piety and educational qualifications of some parish priests who lived among them.

Why the Papacy Established the Inquisition

It was widely believed in the twelfth century that the very peace and security of European society could be guaranteed only if there were uniformity in religious matters. Thus the Catholic Church established the Inquisition to use as a weapon to counter the perceived threats to its spiritual power. The popes understood, as well, that the unchallenged questioning of Catholic teachings would destroy the impressive political power of the church. The threats to both its spiritual and political power had to be eliminated or neutralized at all costs.

In the twelfth century and for many centuries thereafter, diverse views on religion were deemed unthinkable. People believed that the questioning of Catholic teachings would lead to disruptions in daily life, civil strife, social turmoil, and bloodshed.

The Inquisition was designed to prevent such tragedies from occurring. A quasi-legal apparatus with all authority coming from Rome, the Inquisition's objective was to defend traditional Catholic teachings in faith and morals. Originally, the Inquisition was to accomplish its task by intellectual persuasion. Ultimately, the leaders of the Inquisition used severe punishments, even arranging for executions by burning, to intimidate those believed to have veered from the path of official Catholic teachings.

Inquisitors, the men who presided over the inquisitorial courts, were supposed to ferret out heresy—that is, religious views that went against the teachings of the church—and heretics—the holders of those views. The inquisitors' mandate was to bring heretics back into the fold or to remove them from Christian society, for the sake of the greater good, namely social, political, and religious harmony.

Catholicism Versus Protestantism

As more individuals, as well as the increasingly powerful political states of Western Europe, continued to challenge the authority of the church in Rome, both religious and political, Rome fought back. It authorized the Inquisition to use increasingly brutal measures against heretics. It permitted the Inquisition to grow into a very wealthy and politically powerful organization of international importance toward the end of the fifteenth century. As the Inquisition expanded, it ruthlessly overrode its original objective of spreading the faith and bringing stray sheep back to the fold. By the fifteenth century, the Inquisition was infamous for greed, for anti-Semitism, and for the attempted enforcement of thought control.

Although the original Inquisition had its roots in the twelfth century, the Catholic Church did not encounter its most significant challenge until the Protestant Reformation, a massive religious movement that swept across Europe in the 1500s. Those who advocated the "reform" of the Catholic Church wanted to strip it of its wealth, simplify its prac-tices, and bring its rituals more into line with what were believed to be the practices of the early Christians.

Instead of reforming the Catholic Church, however, the Reformation resulted in the establishment of a wide variety of churches in the British Isles, Europe, and Scandinavia. Such diversity was unacceptable to the church, which used the Inquisition as one of its most powerful weapons in combatting the Reformation. And in the Catholic kings of Spain, the church found its staunchest supporters. In fact, the Inquisition assumed its most ferocious form in Spain.

The Spanish Inquisition became even more rigorous than the papacy in pursu-

The Grand Council of the Inquisition. By the fifteenth century, the Inquisition had become a wealthy, greedy, and politically powerful organization that practiced thought control and used increasingly brutal measures to punish heretics.

A Protestant is burned at the stake during the Protestant Reformation, a sixteenth-century religious movement that sought to strip the church of its wealth and simplify its practices.

ing heretics in the sixteenth century. It also sought to achieve *limpieze de sangre,* or purity of blood, as Spanish clerics expressed their idea of racial purity. The pursuit of this goal led to the death or expulsion of a substantial Spanish-Jewish population in 1492 and, later, of a sizable Moorish population.

Long after the sixteenth century, the Inquisition continued its efforts to reduce the influence of the Protestant churches and to ensure the orthodoxy—adherence to established doctrine—of Roman Catholics. In addition, at various times the Inquisition had used its power to hinder the spread of scientific ideas that did not seem to be compatible with the church's interpretation of Scripture and to prevent the public dissemination of literature that was believed to conflict with church teachings.

Whereas in modern times the Inquisition generally has used moral persuasion to maintain religious orthodoxy among Roman Catholics, in the late twelfth century the church believed it had a more global obligation—that is, to behave as the police force of society to control popular religious outbursts. It was in the twelfth century that the Inquisition began.

1 The Establishment of the Inquisition

In order to understand—not to justify—the judgments and practices of the Church in the past, we must take into account the historical and social conditions of those times of intolerance.

Bernard Håring
The Liberty of the Children of God

At the end of the twelfth century the Catholic Church, with its center in Rome, was the most important political and religious institution in Europe. In the words of historian Carl Stephenson, the papacy was "on the verge of establishing a Roman theocracy by combining the spiritual with the temporal headship of the Christian world."[1]

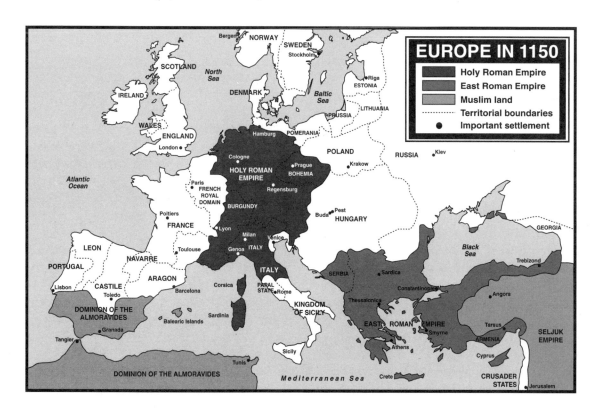

EUROPE IN 1150

Holy Roman Empire
East Roman Empire
Muslim land
.... Territorial boundaries
• Important settlement

With the support of cardinals, bishops, and diplomatic representatives called legates, the pope played a critical role in the religious affairs of Europe. Acting through councils—that is, meetings of church leaders—the pope dictated policy regarding the sacraments, the behavior of the clergy, ecclesiastical government, church finances, and matters of religious orthodoxy.

The pope not only ruled the Papal States, he also intervened aggressively in European politics, deposing kings in what is now Germany and using his authority to control first one side then the other in the continuing disputes between the kings of France and England. The rulers of Poland, Hungary, Portugal, Aragon, and Denmark saw themselves as vassals of the pope.

The pope's power extended down to local churches, which played a dominant role in the lives of virtually everyone in Europe. Except for a tiny Jewish population and the Moors in Spain, all people were born into the Catholic Church, which in the twelfth century had no competitors.

A Catholic bishop consecrates a temple in medieval Europe. While the church wielded tremendous power, church leaders knew that their power could be easily challenged.

Power of the Papacy Threatened

Yet even while they held this central, all-powerful position, the pope and other church leaders knew their power could be easily challenged. Already the church was being criticized, and in some areas people began to turn to other, newer religious ideas. These ideas were considered heretical by the Catholic Church.

Heretical views—that is, religious ideas that differed significantly from the theological positions of the church—took many forms. Heretics might question the nature of the Trinity, the divinity of Jesus or his humanity, the validity of the ideas of the Immaculate Conception and the Virgin Birth, or whether a priest who was out of favor with the church could still perform sacred duties. They might even challenge the authority of the pope to speak on behalf of the entire church.

The papacy was especially fearful of any religious views that defied its authority. If such views gained popularity, the church would begin to lose its power to motivate the people. The pope also feared that kings might join forces with adherents of these views to try to break the authority of the church. Such changes could disrupt all aspects of life, political as well as religious.

All heresies were seen as bad because they threatened the dominance of the church in Rome. This is why heresy was considered as great a threat as treason: "Membership in a heretical sect was a crime both in the eyes of the state and in the eyes of the Church."[2] Treason was understood to mean the withdrawal of a person's allegiance to a sovereign or to the state; heresy was seen as treason against God's teachings.

Heresy and treason were to be punished the same way: traditionally, the punishment for treason was death, so heresy, too, was believed to merit this ultimate punishment. To establish its authority to request the death penalty, the church gradually assumed the right to interfere in the secular lives of the people, taking away the civil freedoms, the property, and even the lives of those judged heretics. It should be noted that the church always maintained appearances by arranging that public executions be carried out by civil authorities, in the name of the state. It is indisputable, however, that many accused heretics died during interrogation or imprisonment at the hands of the Inquisition.

The Cathars

The first indications of the antiheretical fever that would become the Inquisition appeared toward the end of the twelfth century, when the papacy began to hear of and fear a religious sect that emerged in a region of southern France called the Languedoc. Groups of people who called themselves Cathari, an adaptation of the Greek word *katharoi*, meaning pure, claimed that they practiced true primitive Christianity, a pure form of the way that had been taught by Jesus and later institutionalized as the Catholic, or universal, Church.

The Cathars were effective in recruiting converts because their religious leaders traveled around the countryside spreading their doctrine among the peasants. Thus their views were first adopted by many poor, uneducated people. The Cathars became extremely important, however, and their philosophies gained a large following, especially in such towns as Toulouse, Agen, Béziers, and Albi. Thousands joined the Cathars, and many of the converts were well-to-do. These wealthy urban Cathars especially threatened the authority of the church because they were politically active and, like the church itself, a force to be reckoned with in affairs of finance and diplomacy.

The Cathars were indeed heretics who did not adhere to some of the fundamental tenets of the Catholic Church. For example, they did not believe in the spiritual

A heretical religious sect called the Cathars emerged from the Languedoc region in southern France. The sect's success in converting thousands of people greatly alarmed the church.

value of the sacraments of the church, such as communion. Nor did they believe that Jesus of Nazareth was the son of God.

The Cathars believed that their own leaders, preachers they called "perfecti," should follow strict rules of discipline. The perfecti lived lives of extreme asceticism, which included remaining celibate and subsisting on a very limited, vegetarian diet. The perfecti set such high levels of piety that the parish priests, who often yielded quite publicly to the temptations of the flesh, as well as the rich, overbearing bishops appeared unworthy by contrast.

The Cathars believed that at the moment of death the ordinary person could become perfected and find a place in paradise. Those who did not achieve perfec-tion would be doomed to inhabit the bodies of lower animals since the Cathars did not accept the Catholic concepts of hell and purgatory.

The church was alarmed by the substantial following the Cathars had acquired among the people of the Languedoc. The churches in the region emptied, and donations to them began to dry up.

The Episcopal Inquisition

As Catharist views were adopted, they were tacitly supported by many local secular leaders, who extended political protection to the Catharist holy men. Some regional

---

The Episcopal Inquisition

The church asked its bishops to make sure that heresy was rooted out of their districts. In his book History of the Inquisition, *William Harris Rule cites Pope Lucius III's announcement explaining, in 1183, what the papacy intended to accomplish through the episcopal Inquisition.*

"We add, by the advice of the bishops, and on the representation of the Emperor, and the lords of his court, that every bishop shall visit, once or twice every year, himself, or by his archdeacon, or by other qualified persons, those parts of his diocese where it is commonly reported that heretics are living; and shall swear in three or four men of good character and even, if he thinks it desirable, all the people of the neighborhood, binding them, if they can discover where they lead a different life from the faithful in general, to denounce such persons to the archbishop or the archdeacon. The bishop or the archdeacon shall then call the accused before him; and if they do not clear themselves, and follow the custom of the country, or if they relapse, they shall be punished by the judgement of bishops. But if they refuse to swear, they shall at once be judged heretics."

---

aristocrats, like Raymond, count of Toulouse, whose political base was in the center of the areas affected by the Catharist heresy, were also influenced by the new religious ideas. It seemed natural for Raymond and others to support the Cathars when the Cathars in turn had the support of their wealthy neighbors.

This was the kind of development the church most feared: a political alliance with a popular heresy that could undermine the authority of Rome. The situation could not be tolerated. Action was essential against both the Carthars and those who supported them. The Cathars were

> attacking the entire social order of which the Church formed an individual part. No society which has faith in its own values will tolerate public criticism of that kind, and from its first appearance this sort of radical heresy was treated not merely as an error but as a crime.[3]

Innocent III, one of the most powerful of the medieval popes, decided to move against the heretics in the south of France, whom he called the "little foxes that spoil the vines."[4] At first the church tried to use the bishops to control the growth of Catharism. These regional church officials were urged to increase the frequency of their sermons and their pastoral visits to the affected areas. They also were encouraged to try to capture the perfecti. To this end, the bishops were asked to search for evidence that might incriminate local political leaders, showing how they had supported the perfecti and perhaps even hidden them. Because the word "bishop" comes from the Greek *episkopos* (overseer), this initial phase of the papal war on heresy was called the episcopal Inquisition.

Fearing loss of church power and authority, Pope Innocent III ordered the bishops to control the spread of Catharism.

Innocent was not attempting anything new. In 1184 his predecessor, Pope Lucius III, had declared that bishops needed to conduct inquiries into the growth of heresy in their dioceses, or districts, every year. Lucius also ordered the excommunication, or expulsion from church membership, of all heretics. Stripped of the protection of the church, heretics were to be delivered to civil authorities, mayors and other local officials who would punish the offenders. Lucius had proclaimed these orders by means of a papal bull, or official decree, the title of which began, in Latin, *Ad abolendam;* the roots of the English word "abolish" are plain in the original phrase. Generally, Lucius's orders were not carried out during his lifetime.

Innocent III, however, found this mandate to be an easy way of dealing with the growing heresy in Languedoc. According to the historian Fernand Hayward:

> The Church believed that having sacred charge of souls, it could not permit the faithful to be contaminated by such gross errors, especially as those errors proved able to seduce not only simple and unlettered people but even men of high intelligence and education.[5]

From Rome, Innocent demanded that the bishops advise him of their progress in eliminating the Cathars. These reports indicated that the Cathars were increasing both in numbers and in influence among political leaders. In fact, Pierre de Castelnau, the pope's special envoy in Albi, was murdered in 1208, hacked to death, it was reported, by the followers of Count Raymond of Toulouse.

Innocent III preaches war against the Cathars. Despite the huge devastation wrought during the long Albigensian crusade, the Cathars were not destroyed.

The Albigensian Crusade

Innocent III knew he would have to take additional steps to destroy the Cathars. After excommunicating Count Raymond and declaring all his holdings forfeit, the pope called for the start of a religious war to crush the influence of the Cathars. This effort has become known as the Albigensian crusade, after the town of Albi, a major Catharist stronghold. The pope promised to all those who took part in the crusade pardon on earth for their worldly crimes. Innocent also promised the certainty of a crown in heaven to those who truly repented their sins committed on earth.

Crusaders from all over Europe gathered in Languedoc, the Cathars' power base. While many were motivated by Catholic teachings, others were attracted by the prospect of the spoils of war, including such rich trophies as the property of the excommunicated count of Toulouse. The property of heretics was not protected, and as a result whole towns were looted and wasted by the crusaders. The pope's representative in Albi wrote a letter to Innocent in July 1209, describing the destruction of the town of Béziers, another Catharist stronghold caught up in the crusade:

> The attack was launched. The cry was raised, "to arms, to arms!" Within the space of some two or three hours the

moats and the wall were crossed and the city of Béziers was taken; and our men, sparing neither rank nor sex nor age, slew about twenty thousand souls with the edge of the sword; and making a huge slaughter, pillaged and burned the whole city, by reason of God's wrath wonderously kindled against it.[6]

The same envoy later reported to Innocent that at the castle of Brom, a Catharist stronghold,

> the crusaders tore out the eyes of more than one hundred of the defenders, and cut off their noses, leaving only one eye to a single one of the crew, that he might lead all the rest in mockery of our enemies.[7]

Pope Innocent was pleased with the work done by his crusaders. He wrote a letter of appreciation to Simon de Montfort, one of the military leaders of the campaign against Albigensian Cathars:

> Praise and thanks to God for that which he hath mercifully and marvellously wrought through thee, and through others against His most pestilent enemies.[8]

But despite the physical devastation in the Languedoc—the burning of towns and the tearing down of castles—and the killing of thousands of people, the Albigensian crusade did not destroy the Cathars. The crusade, which was to have done its job in a matter of months, instead lasted more than twenty years. The Cathars had enormous support among the peasants, and many were able to hide for long periods of time. Other Catharist leaders fled to Italy and elsewhere, where they continued to spread their religious views. Arms alone could not destroy a powerful idea.

The Inauguration of the Papal Inquisition

So while the Albigensian crusade dragged on, Innocent III developed a second, less local, more powerful weapon for attacking the Cathars. The papal Inquisition was a new legal system under the pope's direct control. To seek out heretics, investigate

An illustration depicts the bloody death of military leader Simon de Montfort during the Albigensian crusade.

The Papal Inquisition

The papal Inquisition, conducted by monks, replaced the episcopal (or bishop-led) Inquisition and was far more effective in finding heretics. In this quote from Gustav Henningsen's book The Inquisition in Early Modern Europe, *we get an idea of the role of the Dominicans.*

"On returning from a journey from Rome in 1217, St. Dominic decided to 'disperse his brothers across all of Christianity to realize the two New Testament principles of communal life and of itinerant and mendicant preaching, principles that a passionate synthesis of thought and action had felicitously marshalled in the ceaseless combat against the heretics of Languedoc.' He would 'work to secure among the community of believers an authentic faith and morals in conformity with Christian hopes and charity.' In the south of France he would work to establish the teaching of the 'Catholic faith and the defense of orthodoxy against those who might imperil it in an effort to inculcate in believers the whole corpus [body] of Christian virtues and practice.'"

St. Dominic oversees the burning of heretical books during the Albigensian crusade. Dominic and his order, the Dominicans, were very effective in ferreting out heresy.

their crimes, and punish them, he appointed inquisitors—powerful officials who would be entirely loyal to the papacy. Most inquisitors were mendicant monks, men who took vows of poverty, chastity, and obedience, and devoted their lives to the service of the church. The mendicants wandered everywhere, begging for their food. They acted as preachers and educators and performed charitable deeds. Their activities were not directed by the abbot of a monastery. Rather, the pope protected the mendicants and gave them special powers, not only of preaching but of hearing confessions and of granting absolution. In return, their loyalty to the pope was total. The monks of two religious orders—the Franciscans and, especially, the Dominicans—played a dominant role in the development of the papal Inquisition.

The Dominican order was established formally in 1216. Associated with the Inquisition throughout the centuries, the Dominicans gained the nickname *Domini canes,* "hounds of God," from this special relationship.

Mendicant Orders Assist in the Fight Against Heresy

Innocent III had great faith in the mendicants. He admired Domingo de Guzman, the Spanish priest now known as St. Dominic, whom he met in Rome. The pope was quick to send Dominic to try to convert the Cathars through preaching and reason. The Dominican order of monks developed among the men who worked with Dominic in southern France until his death in 1221.

The pope sent St. Dominic (pictured) to southern France to convert the Cathars. His order played an important role in the papal Inquisition.

Like Dominic, Francis of Assisi also went to Rome, and Innocent III saw the founder of the Franciscans as another instrument to fight against heresy. The pope was impressed by Francis's profound humility and piety, and he hoped that the example set by his monks, the Order of Friars Minor, would help to win souls away from heresy. As Dominic and his order worked against heresy in France and Spain, so Francis returned to Assisi, where many people followed his example of wandering and preaching, living as they believed Jesus had lived.

At first the Franciscans and the Dominicans followed Pope Innocent's plea "to go humbly in search of heretics and lead them out of error."[9] They tried to

The Franciscans, led by Francis of Assisi (pictured), learned quickly that verbal persuasion alone would not be enough to enforce religious uniformity.

than four hundred leading churchmen—bishops, abbots, and others—addressed the issue of heresy and its suppression. It was agreed at this meeting that banishment and the confiscation of property were acceptable punishments for heretics who refused to return to the teachings of the church.

At the Fourth Lateran Council it was also agreed that heretics would be forbidden to hold public office. In addition, they could not be members of city councils, they were forbidden to appear in courts as witnesses, they could not make wills, and they could not accept inheritances.

That the Lateran Council was able to make these changes shows clearly how closely intertwined the civil and the religious spheres of life were in the thirteenth century. Political leaders knew that if they did not carry out the will of the local inquisitor, they too could be questioned by the inquisitorial courts. In some countries, over the course of time, the distinction between civil and ecclesiastical authority almost ceased to exist.

Extension of Inquisitorial Powers Under Gregory IX

Innocent III was succeeded by his nephew, and the new pope, Gregory IX, increased the powers of the papal Inquisition.

In 1252 the church officially accepted the position that heretics who either refused to recant or returned to their heretical views after punishment could be turned over to civil authorities for execution by burning. This policy was announced formally in a papal bull. Like most such documents, it was known by the

persuade misguided souls to return to the teachings of the Catholic Church. It soon became clear, however, that verbal persuasion alone would not make the Cathars alter their views. Far stronger measures were required to restore religious uniformity in Europe.

In 1215 Innocent III called together the best minds in the church to develop such new approaches. At one in a series of meetings of the Lateran Council, more

Bolstered by Pope Gregory IX, the papal Inquisition became an international ecclesiastical organization of enormous power and influence.

first few words of its Latin text. In *Ad extirpanda,* one of the popes who succeeded Gregory, Innocent IV, recognized and accepted the idea of the death penalty as a punishment for unrepentant heretics. The bull also approved the use of torture by inquisitors to obtain information from suspected heretics.

Strengthened by papal pronouncements, by the early fourteenth century the Inquisition was an international ecclesiastical organization of tremendous power. Its authority to eradicate heresy as well as other crimes against the church was accepted in France, Italy, and parts of Spain, as well as Poland, Germany, Portugal, and Bohemia. In some places the inquisitors were referred to as "Your Religious Majesties," an indication of the awe with which they were regarded.

The rulers of countries monitored by the papal Inquisition were accountable to the resident inquisitors in matters of faith. Upon request, the civil authorities had to carry out the secular responsibilities of

Coercion Versus Persuasion

Historian Gustav Henningsen makes special note of the change that took place in the thinking of the church about heretics in his book The Inquisition in Early Modern Europe.

"[There was a] psychological evolution in which slowly the Church departed from its initial willingness to engage in discussion with heretics in order to persuade them to return to the unity of the faith, and it approached ever more insistently its decision to investigate the heretics in order to classify and publicize their errors and to force them to abjure [swear to have changed their minds] or be handed over to the secular authorities."

Pope Urban V proclaims the papal bull in 1362 condemning heretics. The bull approved the use of torture by inquisitors and recognized the death penalty as a punishment for unrepentant heretics.

the Inquisition. The Inquisition was part of life in much of Europe.

Today, we know a tremendous amount about how the Inquisition functioned, largely because the inquisitors kept elaborate records of their proceedings. Thus data are available on inquisitorial financial interests, the identities of those brought in for questioning, the methods of interrogation, the forms of the court proceedings, and the details of the punishments meted out over the course of centuries.

Vast stores of these meticulous records disappeared during the destruction of inquisitorial prisons during the French Revolution. But enough remains to permit the reconstruction of the history of the proceedings of the inquisitorial courts and the legal system that supported these proceedings.

2 The Structure of the Inquisition

It was reckoned that far less than one prisoner in a thousand left the walls of the Inquisition unscathed, so that it became a proverb that "A man may leave the Inquisition unburned, but he is sure to be singed."

Frederick David Mocatta
The Jews of Spain and Portugal and the Inquisition

By the beginning of the thirteenth century, the church had been prosecuting isolated cases of heresy for hundreds of years. Vatican lawyers used the traditional processes provided by the rules governing the church, which are called canon law. Under canon law, for example, defendants were made aware of the identity of their accusers; trials were open; and only certain kinds of evidence were admissible in court. The church itself was not permitted to cause physical mutilation or to inflict a punishment intended to result in the death of a prisoner being questioned by the Inquisition.

However, the widespread and persistent presence of heresy in southern France, in Italy, and elsewhere called for more stringent procedures to combat this danger to the church. The legal methods developed over the course of the thirteenth century altered dramatically the traditional manner by which the church dealt with heresy.

Instructions to Inquisitors

The new inquisitorial procedures were painstakingly compiled into a number of important instructional books that survive today. These manuals contain information on a variety of subjects. They include directions regarding the organization of an inquisitorial court, instructions for the treatment of heretics, methods of obtaining confessions from prisoners, rules for the disposition of the property of confessed heretics and the punishment of their family members, and a statement of the relationship between the spiritual power of the church and secular power of the government over condemned heretics.

A number of instructional books were considered particularly important. They provided guidance for inquisitors who faced difficult or unusual circumstances, such as persons fanatically determined not to confess to their sins against the church.

Among the most important and earliest of these instruction manuals was *The Directory* by Raymond of Peñafort (later St. Raymond), which was developed for inquisitors in Barcelona and published in 1242. Another was the *Processus inquisitionis*, by Bernard of Caux, published in 1244. Another manual, the *Practica officii inquisitionis* by John of St. Pierre, was written for the inquisitors of Narbonne, France. The *Practica officii inquisitionis* and especially the *Directorium inquisitorum* of Nicholas Eymerich, published in 1360, provided a full range of instructions for inquisitors throughout Europe.

The work of Nicholas Eymerich was particularly well regarded. Eymerich was the inquisitor-general of Aragon for almost forty years, beginning around 1357. He was extremely active both as an inquisitor and as a collector of the laws regarding the Inquisition.

Eymerich's book is a vast compilation of inquisitorial practice, together with examples of how the author investigated heretics and heresy. Eymerich had an extraordinary record of success in extracting confessions from stubborn prisoners, and for many years his directory remained the

standard by which inquisitors judged their own skills in dealing with prisoners in the inquisitorial courts.

An investigation by the Inquisition usually began when an inquisitor and his staff arrived in an area suspected of harboring a large number of heretics. Often the inquisitor received information regarding the presence of such heresy from the bishop of the diocese or another local authority.

Edicts of Faith and Periods of Grace

All the inhabitants of the area were summoned to the main square of the largest town in the area, or to the center of the main village. The summons applied to women as well as to men, to boys above the age of fourteen and to girls above the age of twelve. The inquisitor then addressed the people. His announcement, which was

Members of the inquisitorial court often referred to instruction manuals for assistance regarding the treatment of heretics, especially in difficult or unusual circumstances.

Suspected heretics confess their sins in order to avoid retribution. Many people took advantage of the thirty- or forty-day grace period offered by the inquisitor to confess their sins and inform on others.

called an edict of faith, made it known to the crowd that within a month, or perhaps forty days, a so-called period of grace, the inquisitor and his staff would be available to hear confessions. Such acknowledgments of personal wrongdoing were expected from all who held religious views unacceptable in terms of church dogma, the formally stated principles of Catholic faith and morals. Confessions were also due from anyone who had committed lesser sins such as failing to attend mass, cheating in a business transaction, or committing sexual improprieties. Moreover, the inquisitor expected people to inform on those who held heretical views or had committed lesser sins against the church.

When the people had assembled, the inquisitor informed them that if they voluntarily presented themselves for confession or if they informed on others, their punishments would be relatively light. Anyone later discovered to have sinned or to have withheld information regarding other sinners, however, would be punished severely.

It was extremely important that the church obtain a confession of guilt from suspected sinners because the stated goal of the Inquisition was to help people return to the church. Sinners could be forgiven by confessing their sins and doing penance, and the inquisitors used the carrot-and-stick approach to encourage people to acknowledge their sins during this thirty- or forty-day period. The carrot was the hope of forgiveness, and the stick was the fear of retribution.

During the period of grace, the inquisitors usually stayed behind the scenes. According to historian Fernand Hayward, they preferred to "work in shadow and silence behind the walls of the Holy Office [a reference to inquisitorial prisons], operating only with the help of many secret agents" whom they brought with them to assist in their investigations.[10]

The covert investigators of the Inquisition, called *familiars*, mingled with the people during the period of grace and tried to pick up crumbs of incriminating information that could be used against

Inquisitors pay an unexpected visit to a group of suspected heretics, who are found practicing their heretical beliefs. Following the period of grace, such suspects were rounded up and taken prisoner.

devious heretics. The Inquisition relied on the familiars because it was believed that heretics were particularly skilled at hiding their sins.

The presence of the familiars in an area created an atmosphere of suspicion and fear during the period of grace. As a result, rumors from other places that linked the Inquisition "with terror, nocturnal arrests and torture" probably frightened many people into confessing to sins and making accusations against their neighbors.[11]

People who confessed to minor sins and completed their relatively light punishments, such as frequent attendance at mass or abstinence from meat or wine for a certain period of time, were free to resume their ordinary lives. They could avoid a second encounter with the Inquisition by not committing additional offenses. Those who relapsed into their sinful ways were in danger of much harsher punishments.

Many people took advantage of the period of grace, not only to confess to their own transgressions but also to inform on the activities of their neighbors, whether real or imaginary. The inquisitor listened to all such accusations and determined which were simply cases of malicious gossip and which merited further investigation. They listened particularly closely to accusations of heresy.

Rounding Up Suspects

After the conclusion of the period of grace, the staff of the Inquisition began taking prisoners: people the Inquisition itself suspected of heresy or other crimes, as well as those whose wrongful behavior had been reported by their neighbors.

In the American system of jurisprudence, a person is presumed innocent until proven guilty. Under the inquisitorial system, a person accused of misconduct in matters of religion was presumed to be guilty and immediately lost his or her civil rights. Suspected heretics, traitors in the eyes of both church and state, lost control of their property as well. Spouses and children were released from all obligation to suspected heretics and were encouraged to establish their own innocence by abandoning the person accused.

Because of their presumption of guilt, a person under suspicion of heresy by the Inquisition immediately could be placed in an inquisitorial prison for an indefinite period of time. One man, summoned to appear before the inquisitorial court in Toulouse in 1301, was not released until 1319, although he was not tried for any crime.

Prisoners of the Inquisition

The tremendous secrecy that surrounded activities in the inquisitorial prisons added to the fear with which the institution was regarded. Rumors of physical torture, starvation, and generally inhumane conditions circulated throughout Europe in the fourteenth century and were still being repeated in the twentieth century.

The element of mystery and horror was heightened by the requirement that people who were released from the prisons swore never to reveal what they had experienced while there. The case of Giuseppe Pignanta, a prisoner of the Inquisition in Rome in the late eighteenth century, is a good example. Somehow Pignanta obtained his release and made his way to Amsterdam. In his diary he wrote

that even from this place of relative security, he would not tell what had happened to him in the papal prison because "the terror of the Holy Office is so firmly impressed in his spirit that he trembles only to think about it."[12]

Many of the prisons used by the Inquisition were no better than pestholes. In 1286 a magistrate, or civil official, from Carcassonne, France, complained to the pope about the excesses of the local inquisitors, citing the condition of the prison as an example of their misdeeds: "Some of those cells are so dark and airless that the prisoners cannot discern night from day; and thus they are in continual and complete lack of air or light."[13]

Suspects rounded up by the inquisitors were brought to inquisitorial prisons, where they often endured inhumane conditions and physical torture.

Stringent Treatment Without a Criminal Charge

The conditions of pretrial incarceration depended on the availability of accommodations, the inclination of the inquisitor, the ability of the prisoner's family to supply food, wine, blankets, and other basic needs, and the heinousness of the crime. Often the wealth of the individual played a role in how he or she was treated. Corrupt inquisitors were known to have downgraded the conditions of imprisonment of wealthy people to obtain confessions from those whose property they wished to obtain.

Roman Antecedents

Professor Edward Peters, in his book Inquisition, *makes a convincing argument that the procedures of the Inquisition were not new to Western Europe. Many were based on principles developed during the Roman Empire, acquired the force of precedent by that association, and were more fully practiced by the Holy Office.*

"During the second and third centuries . . . the expanded powers of the magistrate and his expanded responsibilities to inquire into the existence of crimes and the possible identities of their perpetrators removed much of the responsibility from the accuser and greatly diminished his role. . . . The trial itself, as well as the preliminary investigation, originally conducted chiefly by the accuser, came to be conducted entirely by the magistrate. During this same period of profound procedural change in Roman law, the range of public crimes, and subjection of the accused, and in some cases, of witnesses, to torture as a means of interrogation, began to expand upward through Roman society. Hitherto permitted only in the case of slaves, torture could be applied to free citizens in cases of treason, and from the third century on more and more crimes and more and more sorts of people were made routinely subject to it. Thus the routine criminal procedure of the Roman Empire after the second century . . . came to be the inquisitorial procedure, with greatly increased powers and responsibilities of interrogation on the part of the magistrate, the increased use of torture to secure confessions, and the increased use of informers in order to find and bring to trial more and more criminals. The last element of the inquisitorial process, the accusation by the state itself instead of by a private accuser, came to be used as well."

A court of the Spanish Inquisition in session. Such trials were conducted in secret without lawyers, and the accused was never told the specific charge or the identity of the accuser.

A man or woman held in an inquisitorial prison was never told the charge laid against him or her. The accused person was not permitted to have the assistance of a lawyer. Nor did he or she ever learn who had made the accusation. Furthermore, the public was not permitted to attend the proceedings of the Inquisition. All these procedures—the absence of a specific charge, the anonymity of the accuser, the secrecy of the trial—were completely contrary to canon law. But papal bulls governing the Inquisition permitted these procedures. They are the key ingredients that distinguish the Inquisition from other court systems.

The secrecy of the activities preceding an actual trial terrified people. This is how the church hoped to strike dread into the hearts of potential transgressors and keep them faithful to the church.

Accused people were given one preliminary opportunity to clear themselves. They were permitted to tell the inquisitors who among their fellow townspeople had reason to hate them, to be jealous of them, or to expect to benefit if their families were ruined. If the defendants were believed, accusations against them might be dropped. In the cases of wealthy or unpopular defendants, however, even blatantly self-interested testimony for the prosecution often was allowed to stand. And in any event, if other charges remained, the Inquisition would begin its work.

Confession of Sins

The defendant was first asked to confess his or her sins. The Inquisition hoped that the prisoner, who did not know the specific charges, would say more than was necessary, hence revealing information

Inquisitors try various techniques to extract a confession from a suspected heretic. The longer a prisoner withheld information, the more brutal the techniques became.

the inquisitors did not already know. It was also hoped that prisoners would incriminate other people, particularly family members, who were likely to share the views of a father, mother, or other relative.

The inquisitors were patient, advising prisoners to "search their consciences, confess the truth and trust to the mercy of the tribunal."[14] Sometimes people were kept in prison under terrible terms of confinement for many years because of the difficulty of persuading the inquisitors that they were not withholding information.

Seldom, however, were prisoners able to establish their innocence. Poor and illiterate peasants often could not stand up

against the skill and patience—or, ultimately, the "techniques"—used by the Inquisition to elicit confessions. Even wealthy and well-educated prisoners, who had the most to lose and therefore the greatest incentive to establish their innocence, rarely escaped the clutches of the Inquisition. The Dominican monks were formidable adversaries, well trained for their roles as prosecutors or interrogators and as judges.

The small band of followers who accompanied Dominic to the Languedoc early in the thirteenth century expanded over the centuries into a large force of inquisitors who wielded enormous power.

They usually were university-trained men who were armed with special dialectical skills designed to extract confessions from people. According to Pope Innocent IV the inquisitors were to be "forceful in their preaching and full of zeal for their faith, they should be a minimum of forty years of age, wise, mature men capable of asserting their authority."[15]

The monks associated with the Inquisition devoted their lives to rooting out heresy. The famous Franciscan Bernard Delicieux indirectly praised the special skills of those who interrogated the Inquisition's prisoners when he remarked that "if St. Peter and St. Paul had been brought before the tribunal as suspects, they would have been unable to clear themselves completely."[16] Ultimately, then, the inquisitors had both the skill and the authority to use almost any means to obtain confessions.

Some people, terrified of the prospect of being "questioned" at great length by the pope's inquisitors, confessed as soon as they were imprisoned. They received their punishments and eventually were freed.

Other people had no idea why they were being questioned and could not produce answers that satisfied the inquisitors. Other prisoners knew why they were being questioned but tried to protect themselves or their families by remaining silent.

The Use of Torture

The Inquisition then attempted to coerce confessions from these unfortunate people, using an array of torture techniques that ultimately could compel even the bravest and strongest person to make self-incriminating statements. The church fully endorsed the use of torture to extract confessions because heretics were regarded as decoys who enticed fellow Christians into

Complaints to Rome Against Inquisitorial Excesses

The papacy received numerous complaints about overzealous inquisitors, made by local officials on behalf of their constituents. G. G. Coulton, in his book Inquisition and Liberty, *cites one such document.*

"Some of those cells are so dark and airless that the prisoners cannot discern light from day; and thus they are in continual and complete lack of air or light. In other cells there are poor wretches, in wooden stocks or iron chains, who cannot move even for the necessities of nature, nor can they lie except on their backs and on the cold earth; and in such torments, by night and day, they remain daily for long times. The prisoners in other parts of these prisons are deprived not only of light and air but of food also, except the bread of affliction and water, which itself is most grudgingly administered."

everlasting damnation, and to this day the Inquisition is associated with these techniques.

The position had been stated in the twelfth century by Bernard of Clairvaux, who warned that "it would be better that [heretics] were coerced by the sword of that magistrate, who breaketh not the sword in vain, than that they should be suffered to bring many others into their own error."[17]

The confession of guilt was of extreme importance. Not until the inquisitor conducting the trial could announce "Habemus confitentum reum" ("We have a confessed criminal") could the church take action. Therefore, it is not surprising that Nicholas Eymerich wrote:

Too much prudence and firmness can never be employed in the interrogation of a prisoner. The heretics are very cunning in disguising their errors. They affect sanctity, and shed false tears, which might soften the severest judges. An Inquisitor must arm himself against all these tricks, always supposing that they are trying to deceive him.[18]

In this, as in so many other areas, the Inquisition tried to adhere to Eymerich's admonitions.

The Inquisition did not invent the torture of accused criminals. The practice dates back to the Roman Empire and before. When the use of Roman law revived

A Spanish inquisitorial court condemns a man to be burned at the stake. Prisoners who refused to confess or could not produce answers that satisfied the inquisitors often received similar punishments.

in Europe in the twelfth and thirteenth centuries, the practice of obtaining confessions by means of torture reappeared in the civil law courts.

Historian Edward Peters relates that the Romans originally tortured only slaves. Later on, however, "torture could be applied to free citizens in cases of treason, and from the third century on more and more crimes and more and more sorts of people were made routinely subject to it."[19] Eventually all governments in Western Europe in the Middle Ages tortured citizens as part of the judicial process. The courts of the Inquisition followed suit.

The rigorous torture techniques used by the Dominicans on behalf of the Inquisition were highly systematic, and they remained institutionalized long after most governments of Western Europe had become embarrassed to admit publicly that they resorted to such brutal, often fatal, methods of obtaining confessions.

In the early days of the Inquisition, it was considered canonically unsuitable for a man of the cloth to inflict torture. Therefore this chore often fell to the familiars or other lesser members of the retinue of the inquisitor. Eventually, however, the inquisitors themselves often participated in the administration of torture, in part to help maintain the secrecy of what took place in the papal prisons.

Canonical Injunction Against Shedding of Blood

The hypocrisy of the church when it came to torture and shedding blood was striking. For example, the church, as a spiritual body, was strictly forbidden to cause bloodshed. So to adhere to the letter of canon law, the tortures inflicted on prisoners by the Inquisition could cause neither bloodshed nor permanent injury. Nevertheless, prisoners often were injured as a result of inquisitorial interrogations, and death was not an infrequent occurrence.

The banner of the Inquisition includes the symbolic representations of mercy and justice. Despite the claims of this banner, the inquisitors were often merciless in their use of torture.

In 1256 Pope Alexander IV removed this uncomfortable obstacle by giving inquisitors the right to absolve their familiars and themselves from having used excessive zeal in obtaining confessions. And if the prisoner survived the inquisitor's torture and the death penalty was declared, he or she was turned over to the civil authorities for execution. In this way the hands of the church and its courts continued free of official bloodshed.

Canon law stipulated that a prisoner could be tortured only once. The records of the Inquisition show, however, that the Holy Office (as the Inquisition was also called from the middle of the sixteenth century) found a way around this restriction as well. If a torture session ended without a confession, the inquisitor noted in his records that the torture had been "suspended," not concluded. The torture could then resume the next day or the next week without, strictly speaking, violating the rules of the inquisitorial courts.

The inquisitor himself usually did not administer torture. He was, however, required to be present during its infliction. Two inquisitors generally attended torture sessions and interrogated the prisoner. Either the inquisitors or their scribes wrote down everything that was said, both the questions and the statements of the prisoner.

The identity of the person inflicting the torture was hidden from the prisoner. The familiar, or occasionally the inquisitor, who carried out this task was dressed in black and wore a mantle that concealed his face. Only his eyes and mouth appeared through holes in the mantle.

Forms of Torture

The Inquisition used six primary forms of torture to obtain confessions. In the ordeal by water, the prisoner was forced to swallow a quantity of water, either through a funnel-like device that was inserted in the throat, or by slower means: through a piece of cloth stuffed down the throat and wetted, or by pinching the prisoner's nose shut and dripping water slowly down his or her throat.

Prisoners subjected to this form of torture could not breathe because of the presence of the water in the throat and constantly felt that they were choking. The

ordeal by water, which frequently caused the rupture of blood vessels in the victim's throat, was repeated until the prisoner either died or confessed.

In some places this form of torture became even more excruciating. Tightly strapped to a tilted frame that forced the head to be slightly lower than the level of the feet, the prisoner had his or her mouth fixed open with an iron prong, the nostrils plugged, and a long piece of cloth kept over the mouth. The prisoner was always on the verge of asphyxiation.

In a second method of torture, the fire torture, the feet of the prisoner were covered with grease, then slowly brought closer and closer to a source of fire. Finally, if there was no confession, the feet were roasted. Even if the accused person was eventually released, he or she found it difficult to walk. Many people were crippled for life as a result of the application of the fire torture.

Despite a canonical law that forbids the church from causing bloodshed, many forms of torture resulted in serious injury, and even death. (Right) Ordeal by water often caused the rupture of blood vessels in the throat, and was repeated until the victim either died or confessed. (Above) In fire torture, refusal to confess could result in permanent crippling.

Pierre Marsollier, in his *Histoire des Inquisitions*, describes such a proceeding:

> A fierce fire is lit; the prisoner is laid with his feet shackled and turned toward the fire; they are rubbed with lard or grease or any other penetrating and combustible matter. He is thus burned horribly. From time to time a screen is set between his feet and the brazier [the source of fire]; this moment of respite enables the Inquisitor to resume his examination.[20]

A third technique involved the use of the strappado pulley. Regardless of whether the accused person was male or female, all the outer clothing was removed. Then the prisoner's feet were tied together and the arms bound behind the back. The wrists of the prisoner were then attached to a pulley device located several feet above the head.

In this helpless position, the prisoner was raised high above the floor of the torture chamber. To increase the pain, weights sometimes were attached to the prisoner's body. A person who refused to confess was sometimes whipped. More frequently, the victim was dropped to the ground, the sudden release from the top of the torture chamber causing excruciatingly painful dislocations of joints.

The torture chambers of the Inquisition often contained wheels. In this fourth form of extreme coercion, the helpless prisoner, tied to the wheel, was whipped and sometimes battered with hard or sharp tools, which caused tremendous bodily harm.

Inquisitors often resorted to use of the rack, as well, to obtain confessions. The prisoner's arms and legs were attached to rollers at either end of a large piece of wood, or rack. Refusal to incriminate himself or others of unnamed sins caused the torturer to pull the rollers. If they were pulled long and hard enough, the body of the prisoner would be stretched to the point of breaking the joints. Anyone who survived torture by racking was likely to suffer a lifetime of pain if not permanent crippling.

William Lithgow, an Englishman who was captured by the Spanish and tortured on the rack by the Spanish Inquisition at Malaga in 1620, somehow managed to survive and record his harrowing experiences:

> I was by the executioner stripped to the skin, brought to the rack, and then

An illustration depicts a variety of torture techniques, including the use of the strappado pulley.

On the rack, the body of the prisoner was stretched by rollers at both ends, often resulting in broken joints or death.

mounted by him on top of it, where soon after I was hung by the bare shoulders with two small cords, which went under both my arms, running on two rings of iron that were fixed in the wall above my head. Thus being hoisted to the appointed height, the tormentor descended below, and drawing down my legs, through the two sides of the three-planked rack, he tied a cord about each of my ankles and then ascending upon the rack he drew the cords upward, and bending forward with main force my two knees against the two planks, the sinews of my hams burst asunder, and the lids of my knees being crushed, and the cords made fast, I hung so demained [maimed] for a large hour.[21]

Other methods of eliciting confessions included the brodequins. In this procedure, the prisoner had his or her legs clamped between two pieces of wood called brodequins. Then the torturer drove wedges of wood or metal between the leg of the prisoner and the brodequins. A prisoner who delayed in confessing all that the inquisitors wanted to hear might sustain the crushing of all the bones in his or her legs.

The six methods just described were the main tortures used by the Inquisition. There are, however, documented reports of the use of many other methods and devices, including thumbscrews, iron boots, collars and girdles made of inverted nails, and the seating of prisoners on metal stools placed over a slow fire.

Unfortunately, the experience of torture seldom ended the ordeal of a suspected offender. The Inquisition held that confessions obtained through the use of torture were essentially worthless. Thus a person who had confessed under torture was brought before the inquisitor to reaffirm what had been admitted under duress. Some prisoners recanted, or took back, their confessions. In such cases the

An Edict of Faith

When the Inquisition believed there were heretics in a particular town, an edict of faith was announced to the inhabitants, who had been assembled in the main square. This fairly typical edict, taken from Paul Hauben's book The Spanish Inquisition, *was issued at Valencia, Spain, in 1519. The activities mentioned are traditional Jewish religious practices associated with observance of the Sabbath.*

"To all faithful Christians, both men and women, chaplains, friars and priests of every condition, quality and degree: whose attention to this will result in salvation in our Lord Jesus Christ, the true salvation; who are aware that, by means of other edicts and sentences of the Reverend inquisitors, our predecessors, they were warned to appear before them, within a given period, and declare manifest the things which they had seen, known, and heard tell of any person or persons, either alive or dead, who had said or done anything against the holy Catholic Faith; cultivated and observed the law of Moses or the Mohammedan sect [Islam], or the rites and ceremonies of the same; or perpetrated diverse crimes of heresy, observing Friday evenings and Saturdays, changing into clean personal linen on Saturdays, and wearing better clothes than on other days; preparing on Fridays the food for Saturdays, in stewing pans on a small fire, who do not work on Friday evenings and Saturdays, as on other days; and who kindle lights in clean lamps with new wicks."

torture was repeated. Not many prisoners willingly chose to experience this process twice.

The Inquisition tried to suppress all mention in its official records of the use of torture to obtain confessions. That is because the validity of confessions obtained under duress always remained questionable. Clearly, the Inquisition wanted to remove any question regarding the justification in canon law of punishments imposed as a result of recorded confessions. Certainly these punishments, and the tortures that generally preceded them, were among the most awful aspects of the Inquisition.

3 The Spanish Inquisition

If the story of the Inquisition reads sometimes like a tale from a madhouse, we must remember that men do not act thus without some cause. In its own day, apologists laid overwhelming stress on the religious side. To the Spaniard, these bonfires were amongst the greatest of popular festivals because they were acts of faith.

G. G. Coulton,
Inquisition and Liberty

In Spain the Inquisition arrived later and laster longer than anywhere else. Nowhere else was the Inquisition so bloodthirsty; nowhere else were the festivities that surrounded its great events so lavish, so colorful, or so regal.

In Spain, the Inquisition was closely associated with the government and in fact became a department of state. In addition to purity of faith, the Spanish Inquisition required purity of blood as the tests by which an individual could hope to survive and remain on Spanish soil.

The Spanish Inquisition had a broad effect upon Spain as a whole. The country became intellectually sterile and economically backward because the Spanish Inqui-

The long, bloodthirsty Spanish Inquisition had a crippling effect on Spain's intellectual, economic, and cultural growth.

sition assisted the national government in keeping out cultural and other influences from elsewhere in Europe.

Spain became divorced from the rest of Europe because modern books were forbidden from entering Spain. Thus, its universities remained stagnant from a lack of understanding of the changes happening throughout Europe. The country proved unable to keep pace with the growing scientific and intellectual fervor of the early modern world. Unlike England, France, the Netherlands, and Belgium, Spain stumbled into the twentieth century intellectually bankrupt, industrially backward, and agriculturally underdeveloped. Its population had neither the skills to establish independent political institutions nor the capacity to reform the government.

Spain's history in part explains why its Inquisition took on a much more important role than elsewhere. Spain became a national state much later than, for example, England and France. Until the end of the fifteenth century, the country was divided into several smaller kingdoms, most important of which were Aragon and Castile.

Earlier Moorish Control of Spain

Until 1492, when Granada, the last Moorish stronghold in Spain, fell to Spanish soldiers, Spanish land was controlled partly by foreigners. Since the eighth century, much of Spain had been controlled by the Moors, a North African people, who were among the early converts to Islam. The fight to regain Spanish territory from the Moors occurred over the course of several centuries. It was a struggle in which the forces of Christianity were pitted against those of Islam. And even after the fall of Granada and the defeat of the Moors, a large Moorish population, generally agricultural by trade, continued to live in Spain and to cultivate its fields and orchards. The presence of this Muslim contingent, even though its people were poor, served to remind the Spanish of their past

Spaniards battle the Moors in an effort to regain control of Spanish territory in 1492. For seven centuries, much of Spain was controlled by the Islamic Moors.

The sacking of a Jewish synagogue during a medieval pogrom. While Jews suffered severe persecution elsewhere, in fifteenth-century Spain they remained the intellectual, financial, and scientific leaders.

subjugation to the Moors. The Spanish Inquisition became obsessed with eliminating foreign presences within the nation, eventually, in the seventeenth century, insisting that the Moors convert to Christianity or leave the country.

Large Jewish Population in Spain

The Jewish population financially assisted Spain's rulers in taking back Spanish land from the Moors. At the end of the thirteenth century, the large and prosperous Jewish community constituted as much as one-fifth of the total population of about eight million people.

Many Jews had married into the most illustrious Catholic families of Spain. As a result, many leading church and governmental dignitaries in the fifteenth century, including the family of King Ferdinand, who unified the country, could trace their ancestry back to people with Jewish blood.

Its size, wealth, and political as well as social influence made the Hispano-Jewish population unique in Europe. While Jews elsewhere routinely suffered terrible indignities and often were the victims of organized massacres, or pogroms, for long periods of time the Jews of Spain were less subject to such terrors. Despite several bloodthirsty outbursts of anti-Semitism, particularly the gruesome pogroms of 1391 in which many thousands of Jews were killed, the Jews remained the intellectual, financial, and scientific leaders of Spain in the fifteenth century.

But as Spain became a unified country, many of its citizens forgot the services

The Auto-da-Fé

When the Inquisition had finished its work, it announced the punishments determined for those found guilty. This description, taken from Edward Burman's book The Inquisition: The Hammer of Heresy, *is of an extremely lavish auto-da-fé held in Madrid in 1680, in the presence of the Spanish king and his entire court.*

"At Eight O'clock the Procession began. There came thirty Men, carrying Images made in Pasteboard [papier-mâché], as big as Life. Some of these represented those who were dead in Prison, whose Bones were also brought in Trunks, with Flames painted round them; and the rest of the Figures represented those who having escaped the Hands of the Inquisition, were outlawed. These Figures were placed at one End of the Amphitheatre.

After these there came twelve Men and Women, with Poles about their Necks and Torches in their Hands, with Pasteboard Caps three Feet high, on which their Crimes were written, or represented, in different Manners. These were followed by fifty others, having Torches also in their Hands and cloathed with a yellow Sanbenito or Great Coat without Sleeves, with a large St. Andrew's Cross, of a red Colour, before and behind . . . then came the twenty more Criminals, who had relapsed. . . . Those who had given some Tokens of Repentance were to be strangled before they were burnt, but the rest, for having persisted obstinately in their Errors, were to be burnt alive. These wore Linen Sanbenitos, having Devils and Flames painted on them, with Caps after the same Manner; Five or six among them, who were more obstinate than the rest, were gagged to prevent their uttering any blasphemous Tenets. Such as were condemned to die were surrounded, besides the two Familiars, with four or five monks, who were preparing them for Death as they went along."

the Jewish community had provided and turned against the Jewish people. Many resented the tardiness of Spain's unification, in comparison to the other nation-states of Europe, and tried to blame this circumstance on the Jews. In an age of religious intolerance, fear of diversity, and intense superstition, many Spaniards were un-happy about the presence within the country of a large population holding religious views so different from their own. Thus when the assistance rendered during the reconquest of territories from the Moors was no longer needed, the Jewish community became the object of distrust and the victim of overt bigotry.

Religious and racial bigots had been expressing anti-Jewish sentiments for many years in Spain. Alonzo de Espina, a former rabbi who had become a Franciscan friar, wrote *Fortress of the Faith* in 1459. In this book he

> sifted out all the popular legends about Jews who murder Christian children, set fire to Christian houses, put hexes on Christian churches, stab Communion wafers and flog crucifixes, abominate holy images, vomit virtual blasphemies on the Savior and the Apostles and poison the Christian water supply.[22]

Ideas such as these were not new in Europe. They formed the basis of popular stories that had fueled the expulsion of the Jews from England in 1290 and from France in 1309.

The bigots in Spain capitalized on traditional anti-Jewish sentiments and superstitions. The bigots became influential in the Inquisition, using its machinery to destroy Jewish culture in Spain and to seize the enormous wealth of Hispanic Jewry.

The anti-Jewish crusade in Spain in the fifteenth century took two forms. One part was directed against people clearly identified as Jews. The other was directed against people called New Christians, that is, Jews who had become Catholics through baptism.

The New Christians presented a tremendous dilemma for Spanish society.

An illustration depicts Jews murdering a child. Slanderous books depicting such gruesome scenes fueled the religious and racial bigotry that led to the expulsion of the Jews from France and England.

They lived the lives of observant Catholics, attending mass regularly, keeping Catholic symbols in their homes, and raising their children in the Catholic faith. Many took on names that sounded more Spanish than Hebrew.

Doubts about the New Christians arose, however, because many had converted to Catholicism to avoid persecution. Many of their ancestors had been physicians, lawyers, writers, and financiers whose talents were used extensively by the rulers of the various Spanish kingdoms earlier in the fourteenth century. Despite numerous barriers to their progress because of their religion, large numbers of

Actions Against Protestants

The Spanish Inquisition moved against Protestants as well as Jews and Muslims in its attempt to create a "pure" environment in Spain. Diego de Uceda was a Spaniard of the Lutheran faith who was imprisoned, questioned, and condemned by the Spanish Inquisition for his Protestant beliefs. The historian Paul J. Hauben, in his book The Spanish Inquisition, *records the condemnation of Diego de Uceda.*

"We, the Inquisitors find . . . that the accused has committed heresy and apostasy against our Holy Catholic Faith in the following matters and instances:

First, that in speaking of the wicked heretic Friar Martin Luther, Diego de Uceda stated and affirmed that Luther spoke well on the subject of confession; that men need confess only to God and not to the priest. When he was reproved and told that the Church teaches the contrary, Diego de Uceda remained in his Lutheran error.

When a certain person said Luther was a terrible heretic, Uceda replied that not everything Luther said was bad, as for example when he said there should be no images at all, that one should worship only God and the holy Sacrament, that images were for the simple and not for the judicious.

Diego de Uceda communed with and favored heretics. He committed many heresies and errors against the Faith. . . .

On the basis of these and other charges the prosecutor has asked that we pronounce and declare Diego de Uceda to have been and to be an apostate heretic of our Holy Catholic Faith and Christian religion, and to have incurred sentence of major excommunication, confiscation and loss of all property; that we declare his property to belong to the royal treasury as of the day he committed these crimes against the Faith; and that we relax him to the secular arm [for execution]."

Tomás de Torquemada (standing), a decendant of New Christians, was appointed inquisitor-general by the pope and King Ferdinand. He developed the Spanish Inquisition into a form that remained virtually unchanged for four centuries.

these forbears had risen to high positions, even at court. Because many Jews had financial skills, the rulers of the Spanish states employed them as tax collectors and financial advisers.

Jews' success and ability, however, excited resentment and envy in the general population. Many Jews were attacked and their communities destroyed. Still later in the fourteenth century, during pogroms, thugs ransacked the ghettos, isolated sections of towns in which Jews lived. Many people were killed. In 1391, during the worst of these anti-Jewish riots, thousands of Jews were reported to have been killed throughout Spain.

During each of these riots and pogroms, many Jews converted to Catholicism to save themselves and their families. It is reported that during the terrible 1391 riots, so many Jews flocked to the churches to be baptized that the priests ran out of the holy oil used during the ceremony. It was during this period that the chief rabbi of Burgos converted to Catholicism. Seven years later he was ordained archbishop of Burgos. Upon his death he was succeeded in this position by his son.

These anti-Semitic riots, followed by mass conversions of Jews to Christianity, were largely responsible for the creation of the New Christian population in Spain. Once they became converted, New Christians could move openly into professional areas that had been barred to them as Jews. As Christians, they no longer had to live in ghettos. Some married into Old Christian families and became extremely prominent in Spain. Many had offspring who gained very important positions in Spanish church life. Inquisitor-general Tomás de Torquemada and several of his successors were descendants of New Christians.

During the fifteenth century the New Christians prospered greatly and once again aroused envy and hatred. People questioned the sincerity of their conversion to Christianity. As the New Christians became more prominent, rumors increasingly circulated that many secretly maintained the Jewish faith and kept up contacts with the Jewish community.

The historian Frederic David Mocatta writes that in fact it was highly likely that New Christians and Spanish Jews maintained business relationships of long standing. According to Mocatta, "the relations between the converts and their former co-religionists appear to have been of the most intimate nature," and he agrees that the Jews of Spain tried to assist the New Christians "to keep up the clandestine exercise of such rites of Judaism as they still contrived to practice."[23]

If the Inquisition could prove that the conversions of the New Christians represented personal convenience rather than religious conviction, the former Jews and their families could be tried as heretics. New Christians suspected of having "relapsed," or returned to the Jewish faith, were turned over to the Inquisition for questioning. Those so detained lost control of their property and personal wealth, which in many cases was substantial. Often, indeed, greed and religious bigotry motivated the Spanish Inquisition, posing a terrible danger to the New Christian community. This was especially true during the reign of Ferdinand and Isabella, toward the end of the fifteenth century.

King Ferdinand and Queen Isabella

King Ferdinand and his wife, Queen Isabella, were devout Catholics. Isabella especially was strongly influenced by her confessor, or spiritual director, a priest

Torquemada convinced King Ferdinand and Queen Isabella to extend the Inquisition throughout Spain by promising that it would increase their wealth and power over the country.

named Tomás de Torquemada. Torquemada, a Dominican monk, was eager to identify heretics through inquisitorial methods. He wanted to punish them as well as to drive all Jews out of Spain. He believed this would keep the church pure and prevent the souls of true believers from contamination by heretical notions.

Before Spain's unification, the Inquisition had existed in the kingdom of Aragon. In 1478, however, Torquemada succeeded in convincing Ferdinand and Isabella that the Inquisition should be extended to the entire kingdom of Spain. Torquemada argued that once the Inquisition was in place, he could use it to solidify the supremacy of Catholicism in Spanish life. He also tempted Ferdinand and Isabella with the promise that the Inquisition could consolidate their political control over the country and increase the wealth of the crown through confiscations.

King Ferdinand saw great advantages to himself by following Torquemada's reasoning. Although not as devout as Isabella, the king appreciated the enormous financial gains that could be made by confiscating the property of New Christians.

Juan Antonio Llorente, a nineteenth-century Spanish critic of the church, wrote a book in which he condemned King Ferdinand for his greed. According to Llorente:

> The facts prove beyond a doubt that the extirpation of Judaism [in Spain] was not the real cause, but the mere pretext for the establishment of the Inquisition of King Ferdinand. The true motive was to carry on a vigorous system of confiscation against the Jews, and so bring their riches into the hands of the Government.[24]

Although the Inquisition initially acted against New Christians, its ultimate victims were the wealthy members of the Jewish community of Spain.

Spanish Inquisition Usurps Authority of Rome

Once Ferdinand and Isabella had agreed that the Inquisition was necessary, they petitioned Pope Sixtus IV to authorize its establishment. The pope assumed that Rome, as always, would have a major say in developing inquisitorial courts and in nominating the officials who would carry out the work.

But the Spanish Inquisition, with its main court in Madrid, soon began to reject Roman oversight of its activities, particularly in the selection of inquisitors and in the distribution of money obtained through confiscations. For example, the inquisitor-general, Torquemada, was chosen jointly by the king of Spain and the pope, but his successors were selected by Spanish churchmen, approved by the king, and then routinely accepted by the pope. Similarly, the proceeds of confiscations from trials were credited to the royal treasury of Spain, not to Vatican coffers.

Although Sixtus IV complained that his orders were not being followed in Spain, he did not have enough power to challenge a monarchy unwilling to obey papal demands. So Ferdinand gave Torquemada free rein to develop the

A weak pope, Sixtus IV was unable to force the Spanish monarchy, which rejected Roman oversight of its inquisitorial activities, to obey papal demands.

Spanish Inquisition in a form that remained essentially unchanged until the nineteenth century.

The Suprema

The main office of the Inquisition, called the *Suprema*, consisted of the Council of the Inquisition and the inquisitor-general. The Suprema regulated all the functions of the Inquisition including the payment and supervision of a very large staff which ran the inquisitorial courts, its numerous prisons, and other facilities. The Suprema, which also oversaw the maintenance of the archives in which the records of the Spanish Inquisition were saved, became in fact a branch of the Spanish government.

Twenty-one regional inquisitorial offices soon appeared in cities throughout Spain. The inquisitors in these far-flung offices reported all their transactions to the Suprema in Madrid, which preserved their reports with painstaking efficiency. In this way the inquisitor-general monitored and regulated all the proceedings of

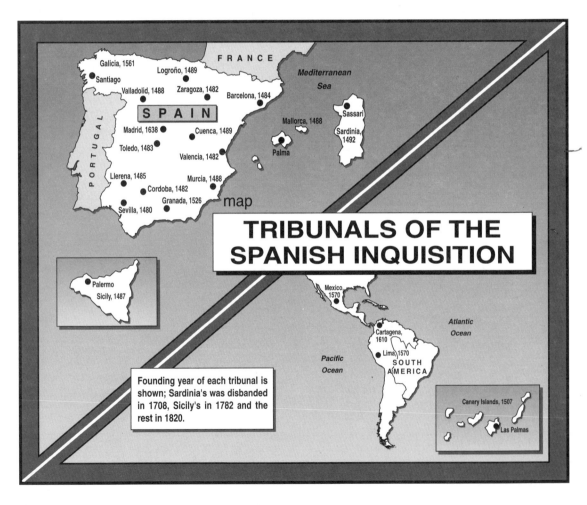

TRIBUNALS OF THE SPANISH INQUISITION

Founding year of each tribunal is shown; Sardinia's was disbanded in 1708, Sicily's in 1782 and the rest in 1820.

the Spanish Inquisition. When Spain established offices of the Inquisition in its overseas empire, these, too, reported directly to the Suprema.

While the Spanish government never became well organized and efficient, the Suprema of the Inquisition continuously grew in importance. So powerful was the Suprema that the historian Gustav Henningsen refers to it as "the only agency of government whose jurisdiction extended throughout all of the Spanish Empire."[25] This organizational strength enabled the Inquisition to move against its victims in a systematic and thorough fashion.

This highly efficient, well-organized court began its attack on the New Christians almost immediately. The cry went up that against suspected "heretics and bad Christians we must wage an ever more merciless war than against the most notorious of infidels."[26] The Inquisition set out to identify these lapsed Christians and to punish them.

Estimates of the number of people who fell victim to the Spanish Inquisition vary wildly. The historian Llorente argues that Torquemada, who died in 1498, presided over one of the most ferocious periods of the inquisitorial court in Spain. According to Llorente, the total number of Torquemada's victims was 8,800 burnt alive, 6,500 whose property was seized by the crown and the Inquisition, and 90,000 given penance in various other ways.

Torquemada Attacks Jewish Community of Spain

Once set in motion against lapsed Christians, the Inquisition began to move against

Jews who refused conversion are burned at the stake during a Spanish auto-da-fé. Torquemada convinced the king and queen that Spain must rid itself of Jews, whom he described as a "source of contamination."

its second group of intended targets, the Jewish community of Spain. Technically the Inquisition had no authority to act against people outside the Catholic religion. The Jews did not fall under its jurisdiction because they had never professed any faith but that described in the Law of Moses. Torquemada, however, was determined to convince Ferdinand and Isabella that it was in the interest of the state to remove from Spain this "source of contamination," to consolidate the national unity that had come to Spain so late in its history.

A slanderous depiction of Jews crucifying a child. The confession of several Jews, under severe torture, to crucifying a four-year-old boy in the Spanish town of La Guardia incited fierce anti-Semitic riots that prompted the expulsion of the Jews from Spain.

Torquemada was able to substantiate these beliefs because, during the trials of relapsed New Christians, stories emerged of interactions between members of the New Christian and Jewish communities. None, however, was sufficiently damning to arouse the monarchs to act against the Jews of Spain. In 1490, however, a converted Jew, Benito Garcia, provided Torquemada with the excuse he needed to achieve his objective.

The La Guardia Case

Garcia, returning from a pilgrimage to the shrine at St. James of Compostela, had stopped overnight at an inn. While he slept, his bags were ransacked by ruffians, who found among his possessions what they identified as a communion wafer, the

kind consecrated by the priest during the celebration of the mass. Questions arose regarding why Garcia had brought the wafer with him from Compostela, instead of consuming it in the usual manner in the course of the mass.

Garcia was dragged before the Inquisition, where he was subjected to the ordeal by water and to strangulation by garrote. Under torture, Garcia admitted that he had relapsed into the Jewish faith and implicated other New Christians, who in turn were taken before the Inquisition. Under torture, these people implicated still others.

Under severe torture, several Jews confessed that on Good Friday, in the central Spanish town of La Guardia, they had crucified a four-year-old boy "in the manner in which the Jews had crucified Jesus Christ."[27] It was reported that the child had been made to carry a cross for several miles, that he had been whipped 5,500 times and that after the ritual murder, the Jews had attempted to cut out his heart.

Although no body was found and no frantic parent reported a missing child, the La Guardia trial dragged on for eighteen months. When news of its sensational contents became known, the trial stirred anti-Jewish diatribes.

Several Jews were found guilty of a variety of crimes associated with the La Guardia case and were delivered by the In-quisition to the local civil authorities to be burned. The unknown child, the supposed victim, became a saint with the name of Cristobal, and chapels in his memory were constructed in the area of La Guardia.

The most important consequence of the La Guardia trial was that it triggered the expulsion of the Jewish population from Spain. Riots following the judgment in the case occurred just six weeks after the surrender of Granada by the Moors in

An Englishwoman Falls Victim to the Spanish Inquisition

Elizabeth Vasconellos, a woman born in Devonshire, had married a man who lived on the island of Jamaica. She was captured by Spanish captains, brought to Spain to appear before the Inquisition in Madrid, and tortured in 1685. Historian Eleanor Hibbert, in her book The End of the Spanish Inquisition, *cites Vasconellos's account of her torture as she gave it fifteen years later to two witnesses in Lisbon, Portugal.*

"During the first week or so [Vasconellos] was given only bread and water and wet straw to lie on. When she was taken before the Inquisitors she declared that she had been brought up as a Protestant and that she would re-main in that religion. They told her that she had ac-cepted the Roman Faith [by marrying a Roman Catholic], and if she denied it she would be sent to the stake.

She was then sent back to her cell, and a month later was again brought before the Inquisitors. Persisting that she was a Protestant she was stripped to the waist and whipped with knotted cords.

Fifteen days later she was once more taken before the Inquisitors. A crucifix was set up and she was com-manded to go down on her knees and worship it, and when she refused to do this was told that she would be burned alive at the next auto-da-fé.

Again she was sent back to her cell, and a month later was brought up for re-examination. This time a more severe punishment was inflicted. Her breast was burned to the bone with a red-hot iron in three places. She was returned to her cell with no ointments or ban-dages to help ease the pain of her wounds."

January 1492. The riots convinced the monarchs that the national well-being depended on ridding the country of its Jews, who, if they remained, would always encourage New Christians in their heretical ways.

Frantic, the Jews of Spain sent letters of appeal to the pope and to Ferdinand and Isabella. Don Isaac Abravanel, a leading figure in the Jewish community and an adviser to King Ferdinand, threw himself on the mercy of the monarchs. On behalf of his coreligionists, he promised to raise the extraordinary sum of 300,000 ducats if the decree demanding that the Jews leave Spain were revoked.

Torquemada learned of Abravanel's visit and heard the king and queen were wavering in their decision. Rushing to the royal palace to prevent the rulers from changing their minds by challenging their faith, Torquemada cried out, "Judas Iscariot sold his master for thirty pieces of silver; you wish to sell him for 300,000 ducats; here he is, take him and sell him."[28]

Abravanel's arguments on behalf of the Jews of Spain were futile in the face of Torquemada's influence. The Edict of Expulsion was signed by both sovereigns on March 31, 1492. The Jews of Spain were given a choice of conversion to Catholicism or exile. Those who refused

Jews bow before Ferdinand and Isabella, offering gifts. Despite the Jewish community's frantic appeals, Torquemada's influence convinced the king and queen that the Jews must be expelled.

The Expulsion of the Jews

The Jews of Spain left amidst heartrending scenes of human misery. Frederic David Mocatta, in his book The Jews of Spain and Portugal and the Inquisition, *captured the anguish they experienced in this passage.*

"Sad and harrowing were the scenes presented in these last days of sojourn in Spain. In most communities visits were paid by the Jews to the tombs of their ancestors, to which they bade a long farewell. In Placencia the Jews made over to the city their cemetery and a considerable tract of adjoining land, under condition that their burial-ground should never be built over; in Vitoria a similar compact was arranged, and in Segovia amid tears and lamentations they removed many of the tomb-stones of their fathers, and carried them with them in their long wanderings. During the whole of that sad month of July were to be seen, along the high-roads of Spain, the long files of the Hebrew people, downcast and sorrowful, some in the decrepitude of age, others in the tenderness of youth, the sick and the halt, the infirm and the weak, included in the common fate. The outcasts wended their weary way under a scorching sun, toiling over the arid, dusty plains, and the rugged mountains, and through the rocky defiles which characterize the Peninsula, conveying with them the scrolls of their holy law, and the few remnants of their wrecked fortunes, and frequently casting a lingering look back towards those dear homes which they were never to see again."

to convert had four months in which to sell their property, put their affairs in order, and prepare to leave the country where their ancestors had lived in relative security for hundreds of years.

The Catholics saw the expulsion as a financial opportunity and bought items from the exiles at fractions of their worth. Many people who had borrowed money from Jewish bankers simply refused to honor their debts. A massive amount of property changed hands during this four-month period. Then, on August 2, 1492, the Jewish population left Spain. Some made their escape to Morocco or Algeria. Others, captured by pirates who prowled the Mediterranean Sea, were sold into slavery. Others were murdered by marauders for the gold they were believed to carry. Still others managed to get as far as Turkey. A few even returned to Spain and were baptized.

Estimates of how many Jews left Spain vary. Some put the number as high as 800,000, others as low as 160,000. The general assumption is that approximately 400,000 Jews left Spain during that tragic summer of 1492. Perhaps 50,000 accepted baptism. The net result of the Edict of Expulsion was that Spain, having driven out a loyal part of its population that had lived in the country for centuries, had seriously depleted its urban middle class and caused untold damage to its commercial sector.

The Edict of Expulsion also created a new group of New Christians who would continue to fuel the inquisitorial fires for hundreds of years. Ironically, the sincerity of the conversions of these New Christians was suspect since so many had accepted baptism in order to remain in Spain. Their names and those of their descendants fill the records of the inquisitorial courts of the sixteenth and seventeenth centuries.

Spanish Inquisition in the New World

The Inquisition also established branches throughout the Spanish empire which, at its height, included Central America, Mexico, many of the Caribbean Islands, and half of South America. There were offices of the Spanish Inquisition in Lima, Mexico City, and elsewhere.

In the New World, the Inquisition followed the practices of the Inquisition in Spain. Spies everywhere reported to the inquisitors on the behavior of the population. What people said, what they ate, and what they wore might reveal damning aspects of their religious practices. The Inquisition in the New World found a wide

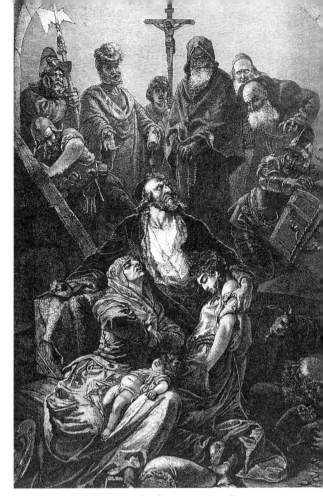

An illustration captures the desperation and suffering of a Jewish family being driven from their home by decree of the Edict of Expulsion.

variety of victims to fill its prisons, and it kept the civil authorities busy burning New Christians and punishing sinners of other descriptions.

Many New Christians in the Americas, particularly those involved in commercial enterprises, had concealed the details of their religious backgrounds, since Spanish citizens with a "taint" of Jewish blood had been forbidden to immigrate to the New World. Because of these New Christians' dealings with merchants in Spain and elsewhere, however, the Inquisition frequently was able to track their activities and locate their new residences.

Once identified, the New Christians in the New World were arrested and tried by the local inquisitorial courts. Many of them were burned by the civil authorities. Their property was confiscated by the Inquisition, and some of the wealth was shipped back to Spain.

The inquisitors in the New World also acted against Christians who committed acts then considered criminal, such as blasphemy, witchcraft, or cohabiting with the native people. The latter crime occurred quite frequently, since Spanish women did not immigrate to the New World in large numbers. The church looked with extreme disfavor on such interaction with the native people, however, and many Spaniards were flogged by the Inquisition for the sin of cohabitation.

Spanish Inquisition Punishes Protestant Sailors

The Spanish Inquisition in the New World was particularly rigorous in its persecution of Protestants, all of whom were considered heretics. The Protestants the Inquisition encountered were primarily sailors from England, who hated the Spanish for nationalist and religious reasons, wanted to harm them commercially, and desired to obtain their wealth. These sailors followed the trail of the Spanish treasure fleets, which twice a year transported huge quantities of gold and silver from the New World back to Spain.

The routes and timing of the movement of treasure fleets varied little from year to year. Such famous mariners of the sixteenth century as Sir Francis Drake and Sir Walter Raleigh tested their wits and their seamanship against the Spanish treasure ships and the warships that guarded them. Any sailor who captured part of this Spanish wealth and brought it back to England would be a national hero.

A few such English adventurers were successful. Many more were not, and those captured were tried as heretics and burned at the stake on orders of the Inquisition in the New World.

English sailors like Sir Walter Raleigh risked capture and execution during daring efforts to seize riches from Spanish treasure fleets.

The Spanish Inquisition in Portugal

Between 1580 and 1640 the government of Spain also controlled the government of Portugal. As a result, it established offices of the Inquisition in Lisbon and several other cities. The courts of the Inquisition quickly moved against the New Christians of Portugal, who had been forced to convert en masse in 1497. It also investigated Spanish Jews who had moved to Portugal as a result of the expulsion of 1492. The story of the Inquisition in Portugal—the trials, the punishments, the burnings, and the confiscations of property—mirrored that of Spain between 1580 and 1640.

Through the strength of its efforts in Spain, the New World, and Portugal, the Spanish Inquisition became the single most important institution in Spanish society. It often rivaled and challenged the authority of the monarch. This was possible because the successors of Ferdinand either were not interested in the empire or, increasingly, were feebleminded and easily dominated by the powerful Dominicans who controlled the Suprema in Madrid.

In fact, by the end of the seventeenth century, no royal order—secular or religious—had the force of law unless it was confirmed by the inquisitors-general. These men also eventually gained control of royal finances. Since the Inquisition in Spain was largely independent of Rome, the character of the inquisitors-general determined church as well as state policy for all lands under the nominal control of the Spanish kings.

These inquisitors understood that they could control the state by controlling the information generally available. Fear of the infection of Protestantism led them in 1570 to forbid Spaniards to study in foreign universities. Similarly, they allowed very few foreigners to study in Spain. And they put a stranglehold on Spanish minds by restricting the content of any field of study that could question the authority of the Bible, including medicine, the natural sciences, philosophy, and the humanities. In the middle of the sixteenth century the church established a list of books of forbidden reading. The list was called the Index and the existence of such a list of proscribed reading was used widely by the Inquisition in Spain to control Catholics' thought.

Ships docking in Spanish ports were searched for contraband, including all books not specifically permitted in the country by the Inquisition. Officers of the Inquisition harassed the ambassadors of foreign countries who were stationed in Madrid. They prevented them from holding religious services and often searched their mail for proscribed reading materials. The result of these policies was that the Inquisition exercised thought control in Spain through the Suprema until the invasion of French armies early in the nineteenth century.

The Auto-da-fé

While the intellectual life of the country ossified, its religious life came to include colorful autos-da-fé, spectacular public announcements of crimes committed by heretics and their designated punishments. These occasions became magnificent ceremonies, staged by the government and

Spanish autos-da-fé were huge, elaborate public ceremonies. Usually held on great feasting days, the events required enormous preparation and drew immense crowds.

intended to impress upon people the power and authority of the Inquisition.

The auto-da-fé in Spain usually was held on a great feast day such as a coronation or perhaps a royal wedding. The time and place of the ceremony were announced a month before the actual event. Enormous preparations followed to ensure the provision of sufficient viewing stands, the preparation of banners and flags, and the invitation of guests from Spain and abroad.

On the day of the auto-da-fé, spectators assembled early to get the best seats. Special viewing was reserved for royalty, for-

eign ambassadors, and other dignitaries. Usually separate seating arrangements were made for the inquisitors and their retinue, identified by the special green flag of the inquisitor, which flew beside their reserved galleries. Other, more humble arrangements provided for the needs of the huge crowds that flocked to the show.

The first event was a parade featuring elaborate costumes and papier-mâché props. A great public mass frequently was held and a sermon delivered. Then the punishments were announced. Those condemned to die were brought into the circle of the assembly dressed in *sanbenitos,*

Heretics condemned to die were brought to the center of the plaza where the king and church leaders had a front-row view of the burnings.

sleeveless garments painted to depict hell, the presumed destination of those who were to die by burning. (The word itself means "unblessed.")

The actual burnings took place in the center of the plaza to permit the king and his entourage as well as the assembled crowds to be caught up in the excitement. These elaborate public ceremonies permitted everyone to participate in and observe the power of the church over the lives of people.

By natural elimination, the number of New Christians burned at these ceremonies decreased while the number of other offenders punished increased in proportion. The inquisitorial records in Madrid indicate that between 1780 and 1820, of the five thousand cases that appeared before the tribunal, only sixteen dealt with crimes associated with New Christians. The autos-da-fé of the Spanish Inquisition had done their work well. They had eliminated what for Spain was the danger of an alien element and had involved the population in complicity with that elimination.

Limpieze de Sangre

Remnants of the Inquisition in Spain lasted until the twentieth century. Although Jews ceased to exist in Spain, the question of *limpieze de sangre*, or purity of blood, still haunted non-Jews. Under this law, descendants of Jews and of Moors were forbidden to hold public office in Spain. By the middle of the sixteenth century, this policy was universally enforced by the Inquisition and extended to social matters such as marriage.

The tradition of searching through bloodlines, though officially abolished in 1835, was so ingrained in the Spanish consciousness that such tests of ethnic purity continued and had to be condemned by the government once again in 1865. Nevertheless, the fear of contaminated blood continued well into the twentieth century. Only in 1992, five hundred years after the expulsion of the Jews from Spain, did King Juan Carlos officially reopen a synagogue in Madrid and extend a formal invitation to the descendants of Jews expelled in the fifteenth century to return to their ancestral land.

This long history of the Spanish Inquisition serves as a reminder of the staying power of intolerance and bigotry, even in the absence of the source of the group against whom those feelings are directed. The Spanish Inquisition also reveals how the original goal to drive out heresy was perverted, being restated in fact if not in written policy in terms of the desire to obtain the wealth of a large population group within Spanish society. The history of the Inquisition in other countries also reflected the desire to achieve objectives other than those originally specified by Pope Innocent III.

4 The Punishment of Sinners

An Auto-da-fé is a sight which fills the spectator with terror and is an awful picture of the last judgement. Such fear and such sentiments should be inspired in the viewer and are fraught with the greatest advantages.

Nicholas Eymerich
Directorium inquisitorum

When the Inquisition had completed its questioning and judgment of accused sinners, it pronounced penances, or acts of contrition. The Holy Office publicly announced the punishments at autos-da-fé all over Europe. In Spain and elsewhere, the dramatic public events were staged in large churches, an open town square, or other large arenas.

Some Punishments of the Inquisition

The Inquisition tried to match the punishment to the crime: Some penances were very mild, others terribly severe. Because people were capable of sinning in so many ways, over the centuries the Inquisition developed and refined a vast array of punishments.

In one of the lightest forms of punishment, a sinner's misdeeds were publicly announced on a series of Sundays, perhaps from the church steps. All the neighbors would know that the person named had missed mass or perhaps uttered a blasphemous word or not paid proper respect to a holy object in the church.

Eventually the Inquisition devised a visual adaptation of this punishment, the wearing of bright yellow crosses on the outer garment. The sinner wore this garment of humiliation while his or her crimes were announced publicly at the local church. A more serious evolution of this punishment involved the wearing of yellow crosses not just on Sundays but for varying lengths of time, perhaps even for the rest of the person's life.

In Spain, the home of the sanbenito, this punishment developed almost into an art form. Like the robes of shame worn by condemned persons in the autos-da-fé, the sanbenitos, or *zamarras*, for daily wear often were painted with red flames, demons, and serpents. In addition to the sleeveless robe, the sinner wore a *coroza*, a high pointed cap decorated in the same way as the sanbenito. Sometimes the Inquisition demanded that the front of the cap bear a sign announcing to the world the reasons for a man's punishment. Women's signs

For punishment by humiliation, sinners were forced to wear a garment with bright yellow crosses during the public announcement of their crimes.

Although the wearing of crosses was supposed to be a relatively minor form of punishment, its public nature made it extremely severe. Even a monsignor of the church remarked on the burdensome nature of this penance:

> The multitude spared neither insults nor mockery to those who bore this token of salvation as a sign of infamy. They were pointed at with the finger of scorn; men avoided their company and refused all alliance with them and their children. In spite of the remonstrances of prelates and Inquisitors' pleading on their behalf, they were treated as pariahs [outcasts].[29]

Eventually the Inquisition agreed to lessen this punishment because of the public reaction to those who wore the bright markings of shame. Thereafter, fewer and fewer people were required to wear crosses over their entire lifetimes.

Cycles of Prayers

The Inquisition frequently required people who had once flirted with heretical ideas to take part in various cycles of prayers, sometimes as many as seven a day. Often the prayers could be recited at home. Sometimes they were said in church, so that they could be monitored by a priest. People who had committed lesser sins could complete these penances in a relatively short time. Some sentences, however, called for the continuation of the prayer cycle throughout the life of the penitent.

Instead of requiring a cycle of prayers, an inquisitor might decide to impose a series of extra fasting days. Historian A. L.

were attached to their veils. If a person died at the hands of the Inquisition, his or her sanbenito was hung in a Dominican church, tagged with the name of the sinner as a warning.

The Inquisition used variations of the wearing of crosses. Malicious gossips wore strips of red cloth, which represented their wicked tongues. Sorcerers, idolaters, and devil worshipers had their clothing emblazoned with grotesque figures that resembled the gargoyles or monstrous creatures that decorated the cathedrals in the Middle Ages.

Maycock notes the case of Pons Roger, who in the thirteenth century was obliged not only to alter his diet permanently, but also to suffer a number of other punishments. Pons Roger was required

> to fast forever from flesh [meat] and eggs, and cheese and all that comes from flesh, except at Easter, Pentecost and Christmas. . . . He is to keep three Lents a year, fasting . . . unless from

Zamarras *were painted with red flames, demons, and serpents to depict hell, the presumed destination of the wearers.*

bodily infirmity or the heat of the weather he shall be dispensed. . . . He is to be beaten with rods on his bare back three Sundays running by the village priest; he is to wear a distinctive dress marked with crosses, to designate him as a former heretic; and to hear Mass every day, if possible, recite seventy Paternosters a day and twenty during the night [say the Lord's Prayer that many times]. . . . Finally, once a month he is to show the parchment on which all this is written to the village priests.[30]

Public Whipping

Sometimes repentant sinners were subjected to public whippings at church to atone for their transgressions. As with other punishments, the suffering due to whipping was intended to serve as a graphic deterrent to those who might be tempted to follow the path of the heretic or to protect others. The following passage provides an indication of what was involved in punishment by flagellation or whipping.

> The penitent came to the church bare footed, in his shirt and drawers, with a taper [candle] in one hand and the executioner's rods [implements to be used in the whipping] in the other. Then he stood or knelt during Mass in a conspicuous place. After the gospel or offertory, or the sermon, if there was one, he laid his taper on the altar and offered the rods to the priest; then he knelt down to be whipped. At the time of the procession, he followed in the same guise after the

A public whipping in medieval Europe. The Spanish Inquisition took this form of punishment to a new extreme with public scourging.

priests and clerks, and was whipped at the last halting-place. As soon as he received his penance, he proclaimed aloud that this was in reward for the faults that he had committed against the Inquisitors and the Inquisition.[31]

Public Scourging

The Spanish Inquisition so refined the practice of flagellation that whipping in church developed into a much more elaborate and dreaded occasion—public scourging. The confessed sinner either walked through the streets or rode on an ass, and during this procession was whipped. The number of lashings varied from one lash to two hundred lashes, and the punishment was meted out to both males and females.

Sometimes crowds gathered to taunt the penitent, throwing objects to add to the suffering. It seems that the age of the confessed sinner did not alter the extent of the punishment—there are records of girls of twelve and women in their seventies having undergone scourging.

Pilgrimages

The Inquisition sometimes sent people on pilgrimages. This form of penance varied from simple but frequent trips to local shrines to longer journeys to the three most famous shrines of Europe—St. James of Compostela in Spain, the Three Kings of Cologne, or Rome itself.

The pilgrim carried a document containing instructions on the places to be visited and any religious exercises to be performed. The document acted as a kind of passport, which was signed by the priest at each shrine where the pilgrim stopped. Thus when a penitent returned from a pilgrimage, he or she had proofs to demonstrate to the Inquisition that all obligations had been fulfilled.

While today the idea of a pilgrimage does not seem especially burdensome, traveling even a few hundred miles from home was a terrible hardship in the Middle Ages. It involved an enormous sacrifice in time and was extremely dangerous. Often it meant starvation for the penitent's family, who would have no money for food in the absence of the breadwinner.

We know from inquisitorial records that the ordering of pilgrimages was used frequently as a form of penance. In 1227 alone, 427 confessed heretics from the Languedoc were ordered to make the pilgrimage to St. James of Compostela, a journey of four hundred miles over the perilous trails of the Pyrenees mountains. Some made the pilgrimage barefoot.

Sentences to Prison Terms

For people whose punishment was a long prison sentence, however, the idea of undertaking a pilgrimage to St. James might well have seemed a welcome alternative.

A pilgrim arrives at the door of a shrine after a long, arduous journey. Pilgrimages of hundreds of miles were sometimes ordered as punishments to sinners.

That is because the same dreary, dank prison that housed suspects before their trials often became their residence for the remainder of their lives.

Theoretically, the official sentence of imprisonment announced by the Inquisition at an auto-da-fé was a life sentence without possibility of parole. In fact, a person could be imprisoned either for a short term or for life.

In the short or light sentence known as the *murus largus*, a person might be confined to his own home, or to an institution such as a convent or hospital, since often the Inquisition did not have enough cells to house all the people it had convicted. Thus some prisoners had the opportunity to join in the communal life of the institution in which they were confined.

The *murus stricturus* was the punishment reserved for those who had committed graver crimes such as attempting to convert others to heretical views or of protecting people they knew to be guilty in this respect. These people were placed permanently in the prisons of the Inquisition, which owned and operated many such facilities. The cells varied in size and shape, but none was intended to ease the suffering of the occupant.

Generally, the cells were very tiny and had no windows. Frequently prisoners were chained to the walls. Sometimes their feet were shackled. Often their nourishment was limited to bread and water. Some prisoners were placed in penitential dungeons, in solitary confinement. Under such harsh circumstances, regardless of the length of the sentence imposed, prisoners often died long before their terms had expired.

Inquisitorial Prisons

People who were sentenced to long prison terms faced the daily torments of incarceration. Even priests were condemned to this form of punishment. Information survives of the sentence contrived for one priest, Fra Tommaso Fabiano. This account is taken from the book History of the Inquisition, *by William Harris Rule.*

"'Fra Tommaso Fabiano di Mileto, sentenced in Rome that crimes may not remain unpunished with a bad example to our neighbors, it is our pleasure that you be walled up in a place surrounded with four walls which place we will cause to be assigned to you; where, with anguish of heart and abundance of tears, you shall bewail your sins and offences committed against the majesty of God, the Holy Mother Church, and the religion of the Father, St. Francis, in which you have made profession.'

[Fra Tommaso had four walls built around him] but with sufficient space to kneel down before a crucifix and an image of the Virgin, this poor man was to be confined, and out of that place he was not to stir, but there suffer anguish of heart, and shed many tears. There was no order given for any door, but only four walls were to be built up around him; and from what is known of those structures, we may suppose that a small opening was to be left above, for food to be dropped down to him. It was what would be called in England 'a little-ease,' where the prisoner was to be kept, to putrefy and expire in his own filth."

Loss of Property

People who were imprisoned generally lost their property. Theoretically, a person in prison had no life of his or her own and therefore ceased to be able to own property. The Inquisition did not generally

Some unlucky prisoners were condemned to life sentences in the dark, dreary inquisitorial prisons.

make provision for the spouses of heretics. It might, however, arrange for their children to receive minimal care.

The inquisitor Eymerich was quite specific in directing his colleagues with regard to providing for the children of heretics:

> The sins of fathers were visited on children; children of heretics were deserving of no other inheritance than poverty and infamy. The Merciful Church might take care of children, binding boys as apprentices to a trade, girls to service, even feeding the last infant or sickly children but she must feed them scantily, that they may be sensible of the visitation, in their own persons, of their father's iniquity [sin]. As for wives, they share the fortunes of their husbands, unless a superior fidelity to the Holy Office should have entitled them to indulgent consideration after the perpetual imprisonment, or the fiery death, of their rejected husbands.[32]

The church hoped that the severity of the punishment it inflicted on heretics' families would deter further heresy.

In the early years of the Inquisition, the confiscated property of heretics was supposed to be destroyed. Pope Innocent IV ordered the destruction of all the houses in the neighborhoods in which heretics had lived, in addition to the heretics' own dwellings.

It seems, however, that this papal order frequently was not executed. Such destruction of property would have caused terrible economic hardship in large regions. If the policy had been carried out, it might well have diminished the cooperation of the civil authorities, whose support the Inquisition required to carry out its work.

After the middle of the fourteenth century, property rarely was destroyed. Instead, property of condemned people was divided among the pope, the Inquisition, and the civil authorities in the area where the heretics had lived.

The Spanish Inquisition found an additional way of turning the punishment of sinners to its financial advantage. Ferdinand of Aragon, the king of Spain at the end of the fifteenth century, had an enormous fleet. Mortality among sailors was high, and Ferdinand always was in need of sailors to keep his ships at sea.

King Ferdinand personally originated the idea of sending confessed sinners, condemned by the Inquisition, to work in the galleys for as long as ten years. In fact, in Spain "condemned to the galleys" was one of the most frequent minor penalties

(Above) Prisoners of the Inquisition were sometimes shackled and given only bread and water. (Right) A family of heretics is condemned to death. Inquisitors showed little mercy for the spouses and children of heretics.

Confiscation of Property

The confiscation of property became a serious matter, not only for the family of the heretic but for all those with whom he had conducted business and for the region in which he lived. Sir Alexander Cardew describes the complexity of the issue in his book A Short History of the Inquisition.

"All debts contracted by heretics and all hypothecations [pledges] and liens given by them to secure loans were void. So serious an element of uncertainty was thus introduced into business transactions that in Florence it became the practice to require the vendor of real estate to furnish security against the possibility of future sentences of confiscation by the Inquisition. No one could be sure of the orthodoxy of the seller of any property, or foresee when he might be involved in some charge of heresy. Even in the case of contracts for personalty, similar security was often demanded, and the interference with business became so serious that in 1283 Pope Martin IV ordered that real property in the hands of bona fide purchasers was not to be seized in the case of an Inquisitorial finding against the seller."

---

assigned to sinners.

By tapping into the manpower at the disposal of the Inquisition, King Ferdinand "found himself a cheap source of labour without having to resort to open slavery."[33] After public sentencing, the new sailors were taken from their towns in chains. Then they were transferred to ships which would be their prisons for the next several years. This practice continued until the middle of the eighteenth century.

Death by Burning

The ultimate punishment of the Inquisition was death by burning. This form of execution was reserved for unrepentant sinners and relapsed heretics. The inquisitor presiding at the auto-da-fé addressed people condemned to death as follows: "We dismiss you from our ecclesiastical forum and abandon you to the secular arm. But we strongly beseech the secular court to mitigate its sentence in such a way as to avoid bloodshed or danger of death."[34] Those words were uttered because the church was ruled by the maxim *ecclesia abhorret a sanguine*, "the church shrinks from blood." The church itself could not be responsible for the shedding of blood.

But everyone present knew that a prisoner turned over to the secular authorities would be burned at the stake almost immediately. The church had simply decided to pass on the responsibility to the secular authorities.

Before a heretic was tied to the stake and the fire was lit, he was given one last opportunity to mitigate the agony of being burned alive:

Godfearing men are sent by the Inquisitors to converse with the doomed offender, to speak to him of the nothingness of this world, the miseries of life, and the glories of heaven. They tell him that since he cannot escape temporal death, he ought to be reconciled with God. If he will not heed their exhortations, he must feel the fire, but if he will confess, be absolved, and receive the host [accept Holy Communion], the Church will graciously receive him to her bosom; and although he must die for the good of his soul, the secular arm will so act that his death shall be moderately easy.[35]

In practical terms, this meant that heretics who confessed to their sins and asked to be received back into the church at the moment before being tied to the stake would be garroted, or strangled. The fires would then be lit, but the bodies burned would be dead.

Death by burning was the ultimate punishment of the Inquisition, reserved for unrepentant sinners and relapsed heretics.

Council of Blood in the Netherlands

In some places heretics were burned in a way that maximized their suffering. In the Netherlands, for example, where the Inquisition was known as the Council of Blood, the burning of heretics had undergone a truly sadistic refinement. Historian Eleanor Hibbert describes this form of torture:

> One exceptionally cruel practice was to burn the tip of the tongue with a

Public executions of heretics provided excitement to the otherwise dull, dreary lives of many common people.

red-hot iron. The swollen tongue was then compressed between two plates of metal which were screwed tightly together. The sufferer was taken to the scaffold where he was to be burned alive. In acute pain, it was very probable that the victim would be unable to suppress his groans which, with his swollen tongue between the pieces of metal, would sound like some strange language. This was intended to add to the amusement of the spectators.[36]

In the Netherlands, where the inquisitorial courts were not run by Dominicans, the punishment of heretics lost all semblance of religious penance. In the middle years of the sixteenth century, animosity between the Protestant Netherlanders and the Catholic soldiers of King Philip II of Spain took on the appearance of a civil war. The Netherlands was in the possession of the duke of Alva, representing the king of Spain, and the duke allowed the ongoing battle between his soldiers and the Protestants of the Low Countries to degenerate into a series of confrontations characterized by acts of great cruelty. The fact that the Inquisition was primarily an ecclesiastical, not a political or military instrument, was disregarded, and the Council of Blood reportedly hanged many people it considered heretics. Many others were beheaded. Once the council had condemned a heretic to die, bloodthirsty, uncontrolled, and vicious soldiers carried out the sentence. All Protestants were considered heretics.

The Portuguese authorities were infamous for the extraordinarily inhumane manner in which they carried out the death penalty. The burning place was near the banks of the Tagus River in Lisbon.

During his reign in the Netherlands, the duke of Alva (seated) did nothing to stop the Council of Blood's brutal torture of Protestants.

The secular authorities erected a stake, which rose twelve feet above the ground and had a crossbar built across it. The doomed person climbed a ladder to this perch and was chained there. If a man refused to repent, the inquisitors announced that he was being left to the devil.

Such an announcement was always a crowd pleaser, for it signaled the opportunity to see a person endure horrible pain. To the modern reader, the frank enjoyment of the physical suffering of others seems inexplicable. But life in those days was cruel in general, and cockfights, the baiting of bears, the whipping and mutila-tion of thieves, and the barbaric punishments of heretics added excitement to an otherwise dull and uncertain existence. William Harris Rule reports:

> On perceiving [that the sinner was be-ing left to the devil], the mob shouted, "Let the dog's beard be trimmed"; that is to say, let his face to be scorched. This was done by tying pieces of furze [a spiny plant] to the end of a long pole, and holding the flaming bush to his face, until it was burnt black. The disfiguration of [the victim's] counte-nance, and his cries for "mercy for the love of God," furnished a great part of

An illustration depicts the hanging and beheading of heretics, two forms of the death penalty used often by the Council of Blood in the Netherlands.

the amusement for the crowd, for whom, if he had been suffering death in a less barbarous way for any criminal offence, would have manifested every appearance of compassion.[37]

When "the beard had been trimmed," the authorities lit a heap of furze at the foot of the stake. On a windless day, the flame would envelop the seat to which the prisoner was tied, and begin to burn his legs. He would be dead in half an hour.

If there was a breeze blowing in from the river, however, the flames could not reach the seat, and the process of dying was prolonged. The victim, in terrible torment, generally retained consciousness for an hour and a half, or even two hours. The witnesses heard his screams of agony "with such delight as could never be produced by any other spectacle."[38] It appears that the authorities arranged the burning to ensure a view for everyone, and to make audible to all the agonizing sounds of dying.

Even the dead did not escape the vigilant arm of the Inquisition. At most autos-da-fé the exhumed bones of condemned heretics, long dead, were carried in formal processions and then burned by the secular authorities.

Punishment of the Dead

The Inquisition was particularly thorough and very successful in investigating and punishing corpses, regardless of the time that had elapsed since the death of the condemned heretic. This high level of performance was possible because the Inquisition kept meticulous records, cross-cataloging names and family relationships, especially when large sums of money or valuable pieces of property were involved. Whenever information came to light regarding a possible instance of heresy, the inquisitors built up a case against the accused and any possible associates.

There are many examples of long-delayed punishments of dead people whose families had inherited property. For example, Arnaud Pungilupos died in 1260, but his body was exhumed and burned in 1301. Similarly, Ernessinde de Foix and her father, Arnaud de Castlebon, were named as heretics in a trial and were condemned thirty years after their deaths. And in 1330 Bernard Arnaud Embrin, who had been dead for seventy-five years, was named a heretic by a distant relative.

Authorities arranged public burnings to ensure that the crowds would be close enough to witness the execution and hear the agonizing screams of the dying.

Embrin's bones were paraded through the streets of Toulouse in an auto-da-fé and then publicly burned.

While the church benefited financially from such delayed punishments, it justified its actions on ecclesiastical grounds; namely, it was necessary to remove the remains of heretics from church cemeteries. It generally was held that those whose sins were not revealed before their deaths had obtained entry to these consecrated grounds fraudulently. The church also wanted to destroy the bones of such heretics so that followers would not be able to gather them and perhaps revere them as holy relics.

So, although the dead heretic escaped burning, his worldly goods did not escape with him. His property became the property of the Holy Office, while his family lost all rights of inheritance.

Very detailed fourteenth-century inquisitorial records demonstrate the zeal of the Holy Office in pursuing heretics in their graves. The meticulous accounts of the proceedings of the inquisitorial court at Toulouse between 1307 and 1323 disclose that of the 930 cases reported during

The greatest carnage by burning during the Inquisition was suffered by Spanish Jews during the late fifteenth and early sixteenth centuries.

this period, 89 were heard against dead men. And if the corpses were found to have been guilty of heresy while alive, their property was confiscated.

People who avoided physical punishment by running away received the same treatment as those who escaped through death: Their guilt was assumed by virtue of their actions. The property of absent heretics was confiscated from remaining family members and was divided according to the custom of the local inquisitorial courts.

Out of need as well as out of greed, the Inquisition kept detailed records of its financial dealings. Most of its expenses had to be paid from the fines and confiscations imposed by the inquisitorial courts. And while the Dominican monks had sworn a vow of poverty, the courts they conducted on behalf of the church often were elaborate and expensive organizations.

The Inquisition paid the salaries of the many nonclerical members of its courts and bore the costs of maintaining the prisons, which were an essential part of its apparatus. Familiars, doctors, scribes, prison guards, and executioners all had to be paid. Thus the Inquisition became highly skilled in exacting the full extent of the punishments it imposed, confiscating the property of the condemned, the dead, and the fugitive alike. In addition, if a heretic died without having completed his penance, his heirs were required to compensate the Inquisition for the debt. The historian G. G. Coulton tells us that "the sum depended entirely on the discretion or the greed of the Inquisitors dealing with the matter."[39]

Experts seem to agree that the greatest carnage by burning at the hands of the Inquisition was suffered by Jews in Spain in the last quarter of the fifteenth century and the first quarter of the sixteenth century. The number of burnings carried out under the orders of the Inquisition generally declined thereafter, in part because so many potential victims had been eliminated.

As the Inquisition became more powerful, it was used increasingly in ways that Dominic, Francis, and the popes of the twelfth and thirteenth centuries had neither foreseen nor contemplated. These medieval saints and pontiffs had hoped to use the power of intellectual persuasion to reclaim the souls of sinners. The punishments of the Inquisition suggest that the church came to believe that this force alone was not sufficient to secure its spiritual domination.

5 Famous Victims of the Inquisition

If a man disputes what you teach, then after a first and second warning, have no more to do with him. You will know that a man of that sort has already lapsed and condemned himself as a sinner.

St. Paul admonishing Titus
Titus 3:10-11

Despite the terrible punishments it inflicted and the terror it inspired, ultimately the Inquisition failed to prevent people from thinking for themselves. Brave men and women questioned the authority of the Inquisition even at the very height of its power. Small religious groups did not cease to form, nor did the development of scientific thought grind to a halt. And perhaps most importantly, the desire of simple, humble people to find their own paths to religious peace was not destroyed.

Challenges to the Inquisition

Challenges increased rapidly during the late 1300s, the 1400s, and especially the 1500s. By then the church in Rome, which had reached the height of its power in the early 1200s, had long been in moral decline. In the words of historian Jeffrey Burton Russell:

> The papacy gradually lost its position at the center of Christian society. It was not that there were no good or able popes, or that there were no theoreticians to defend papal supremacy, but that the political, social, and intellectual climate offered other alternatives and that circumstances arose that made those alternatives seem plausible.[40]

Papal Authority in Decline

The papacy also sustained a series of severe political blows that weakened its authority. Pope Boniface VIII was kidnapped in 1303. Threatened by a violent mob in Rome, Pope Clement V moved the papal see, or headquarters, to Avignon. There it remained, the tool of the kings of France, from 1309 until 1378. This period is known as the "Babylonian captivity," recalling the removal of the ancient Hebrews from their homeland in Palestine to Babylon.

Then from 1378 until 1415, the period known as the Great Schism, there were two popes, one in France and one in

Pope Clement V moved the papal headquarters from Rome to Avignon in 1309, beginning a sixty-nine-year period known as the "Babylonian captivity."

Rome. The spectacle of two religious leaders engaging in political strife and attempting to excommunicate each other greatly decreased respect for the papacy among politicians, scholars, and other people in all walks of life.

The situation became even worse when for a short time there were three popes, one with supporters in Rome, one with supporters in Avignon, and a compromise candidate selected by a council held at Pisa in 1410. Finally, at the end of the fifteenth century, the papacy was marked by an unprecedented level of immorality, inefficiency, and corruption.

These conditions severely threatened the ability of the church to compel obedience to its standards of religious orthodoxy. Nevertheless, the church continued to exercise the great power of the Inquisition to shore up its waning authority. Increasingly, as the church grew weaker, the Inquisition accused of heresy people whose opposition was on political or scientific, not theological, grounds.

This happened partly because in the generations after Innocent III, the church reacted to losses of moral authority by striking back at those deemed responsible. But it was also true that the church did not always control the tool it had created. The Inquisition often became the weapon of men—both corrupt church officials and secular politicians who frequently dominated church affairs—who used the authority of the Holy Office for their own purposes. As a result, many individuals as well as groups fell victim to the Inquisition for reasons only marginally related to the orthodoxy of their religious views.

Even in the early years of the Inquisition, the church had been hypocritical, self-serving, or both in some of its investigations of heresy. But the occasional lapse of the early thirteenth century became a pronounced tendency to excess in the fourteenth century.

The Waldensians

An early example of what was later a common feature of the Inquisition is found in the church's dealings with Peter Waldo, a rich but illiterate merchant of Lyons, France. Around the year 1170 Waldo learned that the Bible had been translated into French. Those around Waldo could now read the Bible to him in his own language. In the past, only those versed in Latin could read it. This meant that ordi-

Peter Waldo and his followers, the Waldensians, were accused of heresy even though their religious ideas were consistent with Christian orthodoxy.

nary Catholics, not just educated priests, began to study the Bible and to teach and preach the word of God without the authority of the church.

Inspired by a new understanding of the lives of the early Christians, Waldo disposed of all his worldly goods, took a vow of poverty, and began to preach on his own. He developed a very large and devoted following, all of whom took vows of poverty and preached in the streets and in other public places.

Peter Waldo and his zealous followers, the Waldensians, or the Poor Men of Lyons, offended the local parish priests as well as the bishop because of their beliefs that any good man had the power to hear confessions, and, eventually, by their rejection of some of the major sacraments of the church. The Waldensians incurred the anger of the universal church, as well, and in 1179 the archbishop of Lyons forbade them to preach. Many were excommunicated, and some were accused as heretics. Some of the Waldensians left France and went to Spain where they continued to preach. There they were imprisoned, tried by inquisitorial courts, and several were burned at the stake in Aragon in 1212.

Among the curious aspects of the case against the Waldensians, however, was that unlike the Cathari, they were not heretics. Their ideas remained well within the mainstream of Christian orthodoxy as they tried to return to a more pure, primitive form of Christianity. In fact, in many ways the views of Peter Waldo foretold those of the Dominicans and Franciscans of the early thirteenth century who became their persecutors.

The Waldensians were dangerous to the church because they followed their own consciences. They refused to accept the rule of obedience, which was critical if the church were to maintain its hold on society. For this independence of spirit, the Poor Men of Lyons were condemned as enemies of the church.

Yet, unlike the Cathari, who eventually were destroyed, the Waldensians lived on in small groups in spite of repeated attempts by the Inquisition to eliminate them. They continued to preach. They survived in clusters in many mountainous regions of Italy well into the time of the Protestant Reformation of the sixteenth century. In fact, there are people alive today who consider themselves Waldensians.

The Fate of the Fraticelli

A second group that gained the enmity of the Inquisition was the Spiritual Franciscans, or Fraticelli (little brothers). They were a branch of the Order of Friars Minor, the Franciscan monks who had helped the Inquisition in its early battles against the Cathars.

The Fraticelli became a great embarrassment to the church because long after their order had become wealthy and powerful, these monks insisted on living by the strict standards of self-denial practiced by Francis of Assisi.

In 1294 the Fraticelli obtained permission from Pope Celestine V to live as hermits, in absolute poverty, beyond the control of the superiors of the order. They wore short, patched, dull-colored habits and they gave no thought to how they would obtain food for the next day. They believed that such concern for personal well-being was contrary to the teachings of St. Francis.

The purity of the faith of the Fraticelli, and their conspicuous poverty—so similar to the lives of the early church fathers—was an open rebuff to the growing wealth and ostentation of the church of the fourteenth century, when many clerical offi-

Papal crusaders attack the Waldensians. Despite repeated attempts to eliminate them, the Waldensians survived.

cials lived in luxury, surrounded by supporters. Frequently bishops and abbots were heavily involved with political concerns, tending to neglect spiritual matters.

Under these circumstances the church was worried about the public contrast between its leaders and the Fraticelli. Finally, in 1317, Pope John XXII, from his see in Avignon, instructed the Inquisition in France to take action to suppress the Fraticelli, whom he considered to be a threat to the religious unity of the church.

The Fraticelli were persecuted for their desire to live as hermits, a life of poverty and simplicity, which contrasted sharply with the life of wealth and luxury lived by church leaders.

Accused of heresy, the Fraticelli were tried by the court of the French Inquisition. Found guilty of holding heretical views, many of the Fraticelli were burned at the stake in Marseilles in 1318. That their religious ideas were in fact strictly accordant with the prevailing orthodoxy of the church was never acknowledged.

The real crime of the Fraticelli was that, like the Waldensians, they had displayed independence of spirit, which imperiled the universal authority of the church. So the church used the Inquisition to destroy them. By portraying the Fraticelli as heretics and troublemakers, the Inquisition was able to convince many people that the removal of these monks would benefit the church.

The Knights Templar

In the fourteenth century the Inquisition strayed still further from its role of enforcing religious orthodoxy. It became a pawn in the struggle between the church and the political leaders of Western Europe. This is most clearly demonstrated in the notorious case of the Knights Templar, a military religious order that gained great importance as a result of its role in the early Crusades. The Templars were in essence a standing army, which protected Christians already in the Holy Land as well as the many pilgrims who traveled there from all over Europe in the twelfth century and most of the thirteenth.

Like the Dominicans and the Franciscans, the Knights Templar owed their allegiance to the pope. This relationship put the Templars outside the control of political rulers and enhanced the power of the church in Rome.

Pope John XXII considered the Fraticelli a threat to the religious unity of the church and ordered that they be removed.

Over the years the Templars became very rich and very powerful, for they acquired a good deal of property in payment for services provided during the Crusades. When Acre, a seaport in what is now northwestern Israel, fell to the Saracens in 1291, most of the Templars in the Holy Land died in its defense. Those who survived retired, first to the island of Cyprus, later taking up residence on their extensive properties scattered throughout Europe. Their wealth and their knowledge of the affairs of the world, which allowed them to play an important role as international bankers, excited the envy of many rulers, in particular, Philip the Fair, king of France. Financial difficulties had compelled Philip to turn over management of the French treasury to the Templars, from whom he also had borrowed a good deal of money.

Philip resented the authority the Catholic Church exercised in French internal affairs, and he came to associate that authority in part with the direct allegiance of the Knights Templar to the pope. Philip thought that if he could control the Knights Templar, he would be able to get his hands on the Templars' wealth, erase his debts, and simultaneously diminish the role of the papacy in the affairs of France. Thus the king began to plot against Jacques de Molay, grand master of the Order of the Knights Templar. First he pressured de Molay to have the king's young son appointed head of

French king Philip the Fair hoped that by gaining control of the Knights Templar he could diminish the role of the Catholic Church in French affairs.

The Inquisition Moves Against the Knights Templar

Jacques de Molay was tortured until he confessed to heresy during the inquisitorial trials of the Knights Templar.

the order. When his efforts were thwarted, however, Philip determined to destroy the order entirely.

Since the Templars' authority derived from the papacy, Philip needed the cooperation of the pope to realize his plan. Oddly enough this assistance proved to be relatively easy to obtain, since the pope, residing in Avignon, was under the control of the king of France.

Pope Clement V, unlike his powerful precedessors Innocent III and Gregory IX, was a very weak pontiff who had been driven out of Rome by rebellious citizens attempting to bring political reform to the papal city. Lacking a political power base of his own, therefore, Clement also lacked the ability to defy Philip the Fair.

Politically impotent and weakened by stomach cancer, Clement V was obliged to listen to charges, first raised by King Philip in 1307, that the Knights Templar were guilty of heresy. Reluctantly, the pope gave instructions to the inquisitor of Paris to move against the knights. In a well-coordinated surprise swoop, almost every Templar in France was arrested. All their homes were searched. The head of the order, Jacques de Molay, and his most important lieutenants in France were thrown into the prison of the Inquisition.

Between 1307 and 1314 the French Inquisition, with the knowledge of the papacy, conducted a series of "scandalous trials" on behalf of the French monarchy. Jacques de Molay himself was tortured into confessing to crimes of heresy. When other Templars saw what had happened to their leader, they too confessed, in the hope of receiving lenient treatment.

However, the inquisitorial records show that in Paris thirty-six knights died from torture, while at Sens, another inquisitorial prison, twenty-five more died under questioning. Ponsard de Gisi, who was questioned at Sens, reported the ordeal:

> Three months before my confession my hands were tied behind my back so tightly that the blood spurted from beneath my nails. . . . [Whereupon I told my inquisitors that] if you subject me to such tortures again, I will deny everything that I now say, I will say anything you like. I am ready to submit to any punishment, provided only that it is short.[41]

De Molay and many other Templars were turned over to the secular authorities and burned at the stake as heretics. The destruction of the Knights Templar shows how a manipulative ruler took advantage of the absence of strong papal control of the operations of the Inquisition and used its powerful machinery to his own ends.

No religious principles were at stake in the case of the Knights Templar. Simple greed dictated the behavior of the king of France. The Inquisition in France, acting under the direction of a weak pope, unable to stand up to a determined king, imposed penalties for the religious crime of heresy against innocent men to obtain their wealth. A hundred years later, the Inquisition in France, again acting in a political rather than a religious capacity, claimed one of its most famous victims, Joan of Arc, the Maid of Orléans.

Joan of Arc

In the early fifteenth century, France was in danger of being completely overrun by the English. The French dauphin, or heir to the throne, was a weak young man who had not been crowned king. The French army was in disarray. Part of the French

A fourteenth-century drawing depicts the Knights Templar being burned at the stake.

forces actively supported the English invaders and their allies, the Burgundians, another French faction, all under the military command of Britain's duke of Bedford. France desperately needed an inspired leader to unify the divided French interests and drive the English out of the country.

In these days of confusion and discouragement, Joan, a French peasant girl, claimed that the voices of saints had urged her to lead the French army against the English. Joan went to the dauphin to convince him that saints Michael, Catherine, and Margaret had selected her to defeat the English. At that time Europe was gripped by witchcraft hysteria, but it was believed that a virgin could not be a witch. Thus Joan, to convince the French leaders that she was not an unnatural being, allowed herself to be examined by a physician.

Having passed this examination, Joan inspired the leaders of the French army to follow her into battle. The result was a surprising series of successes for the militarily untrained teenager. She ably led the French forces against the English in the north of France. Within the space of a few weeks, the Loire Valley, the area south of

Joan of Arc

The nineteenth-century English writer Sir Walter Scott retold the story of Joan of Arc, removing the political overtones that had created Joan in the image of witch, the charge on the basis of which she was burned by the Inquisition. In this passage from The Trial of Joan of Arc, *Scott explains the course of Joan's short career and asserts that she restored honor to France.*

"When Jeanne d'Arc [Joan of Arc] set out from Vaucouleurs in February 1429, the English were everywhere victorious: in occupation of the greater part of the country north of the Loire, including Paris and Rheims, their army was engaged in besieging Orléans. Surrounded by unscrupulous advisers, his coffers empty, and his legitimacy denied by his own mother, the Dauphin's fortunes were at their lowest ebb.

At the time of Jeanne's capture at Compiègne fifteen months later, the picture had changed completely. Orléans had been relieved; the invader had suffered a series of major defeats; much of the occupied territory had been liberated; and Charles [the Dauphin] had been crowned at Rheims. That Jeanne should be brought to trial was a political necessity to her enemies; not only must it be shown that the Dauphin's coronation was invalid, but for the morale of the English army it was essential to prove that [their opponents'] success had a diabolic source."

Joan of Arc is cheered by townspeople after successfully leading French troops to victory against the English in the north of France.

was captured by the leader of the Burgundians, who turned her over to the English.

Joan of Arc fell into the hands of Peter Cauchon, the bishop of Beauvais, who belonged to a political faction that supported the English. Above all else, this devious and ambitious man wanted to be pope. Moreover, he hated his own king, Charles VII, whom he considered a weak monarch. Cauchon hoped that he could fulfill his ambitions by supporting the English, who still controlled parts of France. In 1430 it was not clear that the English would ever be driven out of France.

Joan Tried as a Witch by the French Inquisition

Cauchon believed that if he assisted the English in the highly important political matter of disposing of Joan of Arc, they in turn would be in his debt. Then, when next the papacy fell vacant, Cauchon expected that the English cardinals would vote for him, making possible his election as pope.

The English were glad to cooperate because they saw an opportunity to justify their embarrassing defeats at the hands of a peasant girl by having Joan tried as a dangerous sorceress and heretic. Many Europeans, even educated people, believed that sorcery and witchcraft involved dealing with the devil, which was automatically a heretical act. Such crimes fell under the jurisdiction of the Inquisition in France. So Joan found herself the prisoner of Cauchon, the bishop of Beauvais, accused of being a witch and therefore guilty of the sin of heresy. King Charles VII, for whom

Paris, was cleared of the enemy. With the armies of the duke of Bedford temporarily in retreat, Joan was able to free the city of Orléans, which had long been under English control. From there the road was cleared to the cathedral city of Reims, where the dauphin was crowned as King Charles VII.

Charles VII was reluctant to pursue the English, but Joan was determined to continue the war. In 1430, during a raid, she

Joan is portrayed as a brave heroine in this illustration of the siege of Orléans, the battle that freed the city of Orléans from English control.

she had done so much, found it inconvenient to come to her defense.

Brought into court in chains, Joan was tried by Cauchon and Jean Lemaitre, the vice-inquisitor for all of France. Her trial lasted for nine months, during which every attempt was made to discredit her completely. The condemnation read:

> The said Jeanne, usurping the office of angels, said and affirmed she was sent from God, even in things tending openly to violence and the spilling of human blood, which is absolutely contrary to holiness, and horrible and abominable in all pious minds.[42]

During her trial, Joan freely admitted that she had seen visions of saints who had told her to help drive the English out of France. In the fifteenth century, the church accepted the idea of apparitions

that visited people in the way Joan had described. So her inquisitors were placed in a terrible theological quandary. They had to decide whether Joan's visions were genuine or mere delusions of the devil.

Bishop Beauvais forced the inquisitorial court to make a political decision. Political concerns—that is, the desire of Beauvais to please the English and their Burgundian supporters—overrode theological consistency in the case of Joan of Arc. Found guilty of sorcery and heresy, she was turned over to the local magistrates and burned at the stake in the public square at Rouen in 1431.

On her head a paper crown was placed on which were written the words "Heretic, Relapsed, Apostate, Idolator."[43] An English soldier, witnessing the burning, commented: "We are lost. We have burnt a saint."[44]

It is clear that the Inquisition itself did not feel entirely comfortable with the trial and sentencing of Joan. In 1456, only twenty-five years after her fiery death, Pope Calixtus III quashed the sentence against her. Pope Benedict XV canonized Joan on May 16, 1920.

The Witch-Hunts

Joan of Arc was only one of perhaps as many as a million people, overwhelmingly

During interrogation in an inquisitorial court, Joan claimed that she had seen visions of saints who told her to help drive the English out of France.

Although she was found guilty of sorcery and heresy and burned at the stake in 1431, Joan was later canonized as a saint.

women, who were victimized by the medieval witch-hunt craze. This social phenomenon began late in the fourteenth century and seized the minds and imaginations of Europeans for nearly three hundred years. During this period grave famines and plagues such as the Black Death caused the loss of millions of lives; there were also civil wars and periods of religious strife. As historian Carl Stephenson explains, "Psychologically, the growth of belief in witchcraft may well be explained as resulting from the increased misery and discontent [of these years]."[45]

The Inquisition was not responsible for these vast social, political, and economic dislocations. Nor was it originally responsible for the terrible witch-hunts in which hundreds of thousands of women perished. However, the burning of Joan of Arc as a witch publicly associated the Inquisition with the belief in the existence of witches, and this association continued for centuries.

The Church Studies the Importance of Witchcraft

During the fourteenth century the church assembled a vast collection of information regarding behaviors associated with witchcraft. Stories of evil deeds committed by witches, of their night-flights on broomsticks to meet with the devil at gatherings called witches' sabbats and of pacts made with the devil at these gatherings, filled many shelves of church libraries. At the same time, an important series of theological discussions among church leaders focused on these reported activities. All these developments resulted in linking the idea of sorcery with heresy by Pope John XXII.

From 1330 to 1375 forty-eight trials of witches occurred in Europe, not counting burnings by the Inquisition. From 1375 to

Women convicted of practicing witchcraft are burned at the stake in a German marketplace. It was believed that witches made night-flights on broomsticks and had secret pacts with the devil.

1435, the period during which Joan of Arc was executed, the number of trials increased, in particular, the number of trials in which people were charged with dealings with the devil. Historian Hugh Trevor-Roper notes with some amazement that this craze flourished at the very same time as the appearance of modern scientific thought:

> The merest glance at any report by the acknowledged experts of the times reveals an alarming state of affairs. By their own confession, thousands of old women—and not only old women—had made secret pacts with the Devil, who had now emerged as a great spiritual potentate, the prince of Darkness, bent on recovering his lost empire. Every night these ill-advised ladies were anointing themselves with 'devil's grease', made out of the fat of murdered infants, and thus lubricated, were slipping through cracks and keyholes and up chimneys, mounting on broomsticks or spindles or airborne goats, and flying off on a long and inexpressibly wearisome aerial journey to a diabolical rendezvous, the witches' sabbat. In every country there were hundreds of such sabbats, more numerous and more crowded than race-meetings or fairs.[46]

The Witch Bull of 1484

By the end of the fifteenth century the church clearly recognized the existence of witchcraft as a major factor in European life. Pope Innocent VIII issued his famous *Summis desiderantis affectibus*, otherwise

In 1484 Pope Innocent VIII issued the Witch Bull, condemning the practice of witchcraft and urging the persecution of witches by the Inquisition.

known as the Witch Bull of 1484, in which he described at great length the problems created by witches in German lands:

> Many persons of both sexes, heedless of their own salvation and forsaking the Catholic faith, give themselves over to devils male and female, and by their incantations, charms, and conjurings, and by other abominable superstitions and sortileges [witchcrafts], offenses, crimes and misdeeds, ruin and cause to perish the offspring of women, the foal of animals, the products of the earth, the grapes of vines, and fruits of trees . . . that they afflict and torture with dire pains and anguish, both inter-

Unworthy Priests

The following selection, written by Jan Hus to present his ideas on the efficacy of unworthy priests, is taken from Roland H. Bainton's book The Medieval Church.

"Articles have been brought to me from the monastery of Rockcanny which certain doctors have condemned. The first is that it is not an error to believe that the supreme pontiff does not have the plentitude of power in those matters which pertain to his administration and that if he be in mortal sin he does not have the power to bind and loose.

In the first epistle of John we read that to those who receive him to them gave he the power to become the sons of God. This power meritoriously to edify and spiritually feed is given only to true, not feigned lovers of Christ. From which it follows that no one in mortal sin has such power meritoriously to feed spiritually the sheep of Christ or himself. No simoniac, no concubinous priest, worshipper of idols, no perverse vicar, false pope or cardinals, lovers of the world, false promissors of indulgences, hypocrites, covetous and carnal clerics, addicted to mortal crimes, exalting their own traditions and contemning the law of Christ have any such power. Therefore it is not erroneous or heretical to say that he who in these days is called the supreme pontiff or any other bishop or priest, being in mortal sin, does not have the power or authority to license or the knowledge given to exercise the keys of binding and loosing with regard to the faithful in the Church."

---

nal and external, these men, women, cattle, flocks, herds, and animals, and hinder men from begetting and women from conceiving, and prevent all consummation of marriage. . . . They deny with sacrilegious lips the faith they received in holy baptism; and that, at the instigation of the enemy of mankind [the devil], they do not fear to commit and perpetrate many other abominable offenses and crimes, at the risk of their own souls, to the insult of the divine majesty, and to the pernicious example and scandal of multitudes.[47]

The church used the Inquisition to deal with the increasing reports of witchcraft, taking advantage of inquisitorial procedures and techniques to obtain information from suspects. Inquisitors supplied much of the manpower to conduct the witch-hunts.

Pope Innocent VIII, for example, assigned two Dominican inquisitors, Henry Kramer and Jakob Sprenger, to investigate the witch situation in German territories. In 1486 they wrote a book called *Malleus maleficarum. The Hammer of Witches*, to use the work's English title, became the inquisitorial guidebook for dealing with witchcraft and took on the same importance as Nicholas Eymerich's *Directorium inquisitorum*. Its appearance "established once and for all that the Inquisition was

against witches and its proceedings had the full papal approval."[48]

The Catholic Church continued to use the courts of the Inquisition to persecute witches well into the seventeenth century. It should be noted, however, that witch-hunts took place no less viciously in Protestant countries. Both Martin Luther and the French reformer John Calvin "believed in the sabbat and night-flights as firmly as any fifteenth-century Inquisitor."[49]

Although in administering the Inquisition the clergy increasingly abandoned the high standards established by Pope Innocent III, some people tried to reform the Catholic Church from within and to preserve it from its enemies. Many of these reformers were viewed as troublemakers, however, and their advice was ignored. Thus they fell victim to the Inquisition. There was, for instance, the famous and unfortunate case of Jan Hus.

Bohemian priest Jan Hus protested the wealth and worldliness of the church clergy in his writings, beliefs for which he was condemned as a heretic.

Jan Hus, Bohemian Priest

Jan Hus was a Bohemian priest who was described as a "man of fearless temper, blameless life and kindly nature."[50] He was associated with the Bethlehem Chapel in the city of Prague, which had been endowed by a group of men who were interested in preaching the importance of living a simple Christian life. There he became a very popular preacher and had a wide following among the common people.

While his religious views remained largely orthodox, Hus's writings protested the worldliness of the clergy, especially the pope, who lived in great luxury, wore elegant clothing, and traveled with a great show of pomp and ceremony.

Hus also deplored many church practices, which he saw as abuses of the people's trust. For example, the church owned half the land of Bohemia, yet taxed the peasants so heavily they could not feed their families. Hus also opposed the practice of simony, the sale and purchase of church offices. (Much as entrepreneurs today invest in a seat on a stock exchange or a license to sell liquor, expecting to improve their chances of making money, a man in medieval times would buy, for example, a bishopric for the economic benefits it offered.) Hus also opposed the claim of papal supremacy in matters of faith and morals; that is, he did not believe that the pope's word should outweigh that of the councils of the church.

Hus read ecclesiastical literature extensively and came to the conclusion that heresy should not be tried by the church courts. He also believed that the true overlordship of the church belonged only to the elect, the true believers who lived the humble, simple lives of the early Christians.

In 1415 Hus was invited under safe conduct to attend a general church council at Constance to discuss his ideas. When he arrived in the German city, instead of being warmly received, as he had anticipated, Hus was thrown into prison where he was kept for many months. The council believed he was a dangerous heretic because many church leaders saw his criticisms of clerical and institutional abuses as an attack against the entire body of the Catholic Church.

The council turned itself into an inquisitorial court before which Hus was permitted to defend his ideas. The inquisitors tried to show that his ideas were iden-

tical to those of the English reformer John Wycliffe, who had already been declared heretical by the council.

Hus Is Condemned as a Heretic

But Hus stood his ground against the inquisitors and finally announced to them that he would not commit perjury to save his life. The inquisitorial court condemned him as an obstinate heretic, degraded him from the priesthood—that is, stripped him of clerical office—and turned him over to Duke Louis of the Palatinate. The German nobleman delivered Hus to the executioners, and he was burned at the stake on July 6, 1415. The officials scattered his ashes so that no relics of Hus could be returned to Bohemia.

The manner of Hus's death was recorded for posterity. When the executioner lit the fire, the

> master immediately began to sing. . . . And when he began to sing the third time, the wind blew the flame in his face. And thus praying within himself and moving his lips and the head, he expired in the Lord. . . . He seemed to move before he actually died for about the time one can quickly recite "our Father" two or at most three times.[51]

Although the Inquisition destroyed the body of Jan Hus, it did not silence his views, and in the end Hus achieved victory over the Inquisition. The Bohemian population took no notice of his excommunication and honored him as a national hero. Indeed, his death became closely associ-

Hus defends his teachings before the Council of Constance. Unwilling to retract his beliefs, Hus was stripped of his priesthood and burned at the stake in 1415.

ated with the Bohemian Church and with Bohemian nationalism. In the Hussite wars of the fifteenth century, inspired by the independent stand taken by Hus, the Bohemian Church established its complete independence from Rome, which never was able thereafter to set up an inquisitorial court in Bohemia. Protestants all over northern Europe claimed Hus as their first martyr.

Girolamo Savonarola

Girolamo Savonarola, like Jan Hus, attempted to bring about reforms within the church. An Italian Dominican monk who challenged the financial dealings and the worldliness of the church during the Renaissance, Savonarola paid for his reforming zeal with his life. The worldliness Savonarola protested is described by historian Barbara Tuchman in the following passage:

> Under the heady humanism of the Renaissance, the popes . . . adopted as their own the values and style of the piratical princes of the Italian city-states. Opulent, elegant, unprincipled and endlessly at odds with each other, the rulers of Italian life were, by reason of their disunity and limited territorial scope, no more than potentates of discord. In reproducing their avarice and luxury, the six popes [including Alexander VI, the pontiff

whom Girolamo angered] did no better than their models, and because of their superior status, usually worse.[52]

Savonarola was not a heretic; his religious ideas conformed to the dogmas of the church in the late fifteenth century. He wanted the papacy to remember its spiritual charge and to forsake its worldly possessions at the same time that he wanted his fellow Christians to strive for purity in their own lives.

Reforms in Florence

For a time Savonarola was successful. Great bonfires were built in the streets of Florence in which "vanities"—ornaments, fashionable clothings, secular books, and games—were burned. Then, when the Florentines drove out the ruling Medici family and attempted to reestablish the old republican form of government, Savonarola became a virtual dictator.

In his reforming zeal, however, Savonarola fell foul of Alexander VI, one of the most worldly and immoral pontiffs ever to sit on the throne of Peter. Fearing that the zeal for social reform inspired by Savonarola in Florence could cause him harm, Alexander tried to bribe the monk by offering to make him a cardinal. Savonarola refused the bribe and was excommunicated. Alexander then ordered that the Dominican be tried by the Inquisition of Florence.

Under extreme torture Savonarola confessed to seeing visions. The Inquisition found him guilty of holding heretical views, although his real offense was having denied papal authority to control his min-

An illustration depicts Alexander VI as a hideous monster, representing the corruptness of the worldly, immoral pope.

istry. Savonarola was turned over to the secular authorities, who burned him at the stake in 1498.

The Inquisition Is Used to Combat Modern Scientific Ideas

The century that saw the executions of Jan Hus and Girolamo Savonarola also saw the dawn of the scientific age in Europe. Many of the ideas of the new thinkers appeared to conflict with the Bible, especially with church teachings regarding the nature of the universe.

Church leaders used the Inquisition to try to muzzle scientific inquiry just as they had used it to try to stamp out heresy and political opposition. They feared that independent thinking in the realm of science would further undermine the power of the Catholic Church. The Bible was held to be the final authority regarding all aspects of human knowledge, including such scientific issues as the relationship of the earth to the sun. If, however, the Bible were proved to be incorrect in any of

these areas, it could be challenged in other matters as well. So the Inquisition conducted trials of scientists.

Giordano Bruno

Giordano Bruno was one of the thinkers whose views challenged the church. A celebrated philosopher, astronomer, and mathematician as well as the author of many works on religion and the occult, Bruno was a member of the Dominican order. He lived at San Domenico Maggiore in Naples in the late sixteenth century. Unable to accept the limitations placed by the church

After being convicted for disobedience to papal authority, Girolamo Savonarola and his followers are burned at the stake in 1498.

on his readings and on his thinking, Bruno eventually left the order and ceased to claim to be a Catholic. He fled Italy and traveled widely in Switzerland, France, Germany, and England.

In Bruno's important works regarding the nature of the universe, which were published outside Italy, he discussed the movement of the earth around the sun.

Giordano Bruno's works concerning the nature of the universe contradicted church teachings. Like Savonarola and others, Bruno was executed at the hands of the Inquisition for his independent views.

This notion was contrary to church teachings, which favored the geocentric model, in which the earth was the center of the universe. He also suggested that the Bible should be followed for its moral teachings, not as a source of scientific information.

Bruno believed that the Inquisition would not be interested in him because he had left the Dominican order. So when his friend Giovanni Mocenego, an important politician in Venice, invited him to come home in 1591, Bruno decided it would be safe to return to Italy.

Unfortunately, Bruno had misjudged the extent of the Italian Inquisition's attention to the development of his ideas and to his writings. He was thrown into the inquisitorial prison in Venice in 1592, where he admitted to several minor errors in his thinking.

These admissions did not satisfy officials of the Inquisition in Rome, who demanded his extradition. In 1593 Bruno entered the jail of the Roman Inquisition, where he underwent six years of additional questioning and was ordered to retract all his views regarding the movement of the planets. This he refused to do.

Bruno was tried and found guilty of heresy, but he told his inquisitors, "Perhaps your fear in passing judgment is greater than mine in receiving it."[53] He was delivered to the secular authorities in Rome and taken to the public square called Campo di Fiori, or Field of Flowers. His tongue was put in a gag to prevent him from speaking to the crowds. On February 17, 1600, one of the first scientific scholars of Europe was burned at the stake.

Colleagues of Bruno also fell under the watchful eye of the Italian Inquisition. Later in the seventeenth century, another famous scientist, Galileo Galilei, temporarily lost his freedom and almost lost his life because he, like Bruno, challenged traditional church teachings regarding the nature of the universe. A mathematician and astronomer, as well as a physicist, Galileo is considered by many to be the founder of the experimental method of scientific inquiry.

Galileo taught mathematics in Florence under the protection of the city's grand duke. In his teaching, Galileo dealt with the dangerous question of whether the geocentric theory of the universe needed to be replaced by the model in which the earth and planets travel around the sun—the heliocentric theory, as suggested more than a hundred years earlier by the Polish astronomer Nicolaus Copernicus.

Galileo strongly defended the Copernican position, although it was contrary to contemporary church teachings, which were said to be based on Scriptures. It was possible, Galileo wrote in 1615, to reconcile the two positions:

> The way in which I could quickly and surely demonstrate that Copernicus' position is not contrary to the Scriptures would be to show with a thousand proofs that it is true, and that the opposite cannot hold good; thus, since two truths cannot contradict each other, it is necessary that both his theory and the Scriptures are in agreement.[54]

The Inquisition was not willing to accept Galileo's position any more than it had been willing to consider the ideas of Giordano Bruno. Galileo also angered the church because of his "obstinacy in mixing the sacred and profane sciences and

The church was angered by Galileo Galilei's works, which suggested that the geocentric theory of the universe, taught by the church, needed to be replaced by the heliocentric theory.

in setting himself up as a commentator on Holy Scripture."[55]

Galileo's offense was the presumption to comment on the Scriptures in his writings and teachings without first obtaining the permission of the church. Pope Urban VIII ordered the inquisitors in Rome to review Galileo's work and report their findings to the Vatican, to determine whether the scientist should be tried as a heretic.

Galileo's Works Condemned by the Inquisition

Galileo's work was condemned. He was called to Rome in 1632 to appear before

Galileo appears before an inquisitorial court in Rome, where he was forced to retract his opinion and agree to stop teaching Copernican, or heliocentric, principles.

the Inquisition when he was sixty-eight years old and ailing. After discussions with the inquisitors, Galileo agreed to stop teaching Copernican principles. Instead, he wrote the gist of them in a work called *The Dialogues*, in which three people discuss the heliocentric view of the universe. Again he was summoned to Rome to appear before the Holy Office. There was a second trial by the Inquisition, during which the inquisitors apparently subjected the famous astronomer to intellectual, though not physical, torture. Galileo wrote about his experiences to a friend:

At last, as a true Catholic, I was obliged to retract my opinion, and, by way of penalty, my Dialogue was prohibited [banned from publication]; and after five months I was dismissed from Rome, and, as the pestilence [Black Plague] was then raging in Florence, with generous pity, the house of the dearest friend I had in Siena, [Monsignor] Archbishop Piccolomini, was appointed to be my prison. . . . After about five months, when the pestilence had ceased in my native place, in the beginning of December in the present year, 1633, His Holiness [the pope] permitted me to dwell within the narrow limits of that house I love so well, in the freedom of the open country, I therefore returned to the village of Ballosguardo, and thence to Arcetri; where I still am, breathing the salubrious [healthful] air, not far from my own dear Florence. Farewell.[56]

In 1633 Galileo was condemned to house arrest in Florence for the rest of his life, but his case did not end there. Over the centuries the Inquisition continued to review the issues he had raised in the seventeenth century. As recently as 1984 a commission appointed by the church tried to make Galileo's teachings acceptable in the eyes of the church and deliberated on a possible resolution of the issues he had raised. In 1993 the church agreed that it was possible to reconcile the views of Galileo with those of the church. But Galileo still has not been rehabilitated by the church.

The fates of these famous victims of the Inquisition—the Waldensians, the Fraticelli, the Knights Templar, Jan Hus, Joan of Arc, and the others—illustrate the wide net cast by the Inquisition over the population of Western Europe. They also illustrate how an institution mandated to uphold a principle, namely religious uniformity, was subverted by plainly unspiritual interests, namely greed and political expediency. In failing to be true to its stated purpose, the Inquisition contributed to the very downfall of the church whose universality it had been established to defend.

Chapter

6 The Gradual End of the Inquisition

Happy indiscretion of the judges of the Holy Office, its probes entered between marrow and nerve into the deepest secrets of the conscious and unconscious. For an in-depth history of human behavior, for a global psychoanalysis of society, it is not at all certain whether our own age will bequeath to its successors a documentation of equal value.

Pierre Chaunu, historian, quoted in *The Inquisition in Early Modern Europe*

The Inquisition and its influence did not end suddenly at a specific date. Instead, over a period of more than a century, in different places, most formal institutions of the Inquisition, such as its prisons and its investigations into religious orthodoxy, gradually disappeared, having lost their powers of intimidation as a result of wars and disuse.

The most dramatic, most decisive intellectual attack on the fundamental principles of the Inquisition came with the French Revolution of 1789. Many French people believed that the Catholic Church and its powerful judicial arm, the Inquisition, were in league with the king and his court to prevent the emergence of liberal ideas and the democratization of French government. They believed

As they swept across Europe, French soldiers spread the revolutionary ideals of religious freedom, political justice, and the equality of people.

Spaniards rejoice as prisoners are released by French soldiers in this painting of the destruction of the Inquisition in Barcelona.

that not only in France but throughout Europe this alliance between the church and royalist interests acted as a barrier to the practice of new ideas regarding religious freedom, political justice, and the equality of people.

As the citizen soldiers of France swept across much of Western Europe into Spain, Italy, Austria, Prussia, and the Low Countries, they carried with them the revolutionary doctrines of religious tolerance and the freedom of people of all faiths to worship as they wished. And they put into effect in France what they preached

abroad. As a result of the French Revolution, for the first time, the Jews of France were recognized as citizens, along with Catholics and Protestants, and professional opportunities were now open to them for the first time on an equal basis with their fellow citizens.

These ideas were a dramatic departure from the principles that had governed much of Western thought for two thousand years. In the past, individualists had been seen as a danger to society. They were hunted down, silenced, or destroyed. Suddenly, the possibility and the reason-

Freedom of the Press as a Weapon Against the Inquisition

The poet John Milton (1608-1674) was one of the great English writers of all time. He defended the principles of free speech and free press, which were valued if not always protected in his country. In his famous work Areopagitica, *he condemns the Inquisition's attempt to control freedom of expression.*

"The Popes of Rome, engrossing what they pleased of political rule into their own hands, extended their dominion over men's eyes, as they had before over their judgments, burning and prohibiting to be read what they fancied not . . . until the Council of Trent and the Spanish Inquisition engendering together brought forth or perfected those Catalogues and expurging Indexes that rake through the entrails of many an old good author, with a violation worse than any could be offered to his tomb. Nor did they stay in matters heretical, but any subject that was not to their palate, they either condemned in a prohibition, or had it straight into the new Purgatory of an Index. To fill up the measure of that encroachment their last invention was to ordain that no book, pamphlet, or paper should be printed (as if St. Peter had bequested them the keys of the press also out of paradise) unless it were approved and licensed under the hands of two or three glutton friars."

English poet John Milton, a champion of the principles of free speech and freedom of the press, attacked the Inquisition's attempt to control freedom of expression.

ableness of the coexistence of diverse ideas were thrust on the human conscience.

Inquisitorial Institutions Destroyed by French

What they proclaimed essential for French people, the soldiers of the Revolution imposed wherever French armies were successful. Moreover, French soldiers attacked the institutions of the Inquisition whenever they came across them. This was particularly true in Spain and in Italy, where the Inquisition had lasted the longest. French troops destroyed inquisitorial prisons, freed their inmates, humili-

Napoléon Bonaparte ordered French troops to seize the Palace of the Inquisition in Madrid, where they discovered prison cells, torture chambers, and horrific instruments of torture.

ated inquisitors, and captured cartloads of documents. Those they did not destroy were placed in secure places, to be used later as evidence of crimes committed by the church.

After the French invasion of Spain, Napoléon Bonaparte set up his military headquarters not far from the inquisitorial prison in Madrid. He gave specific instructions to his troops to seize the offices of the Inquisition, the inquisitors, their papers, and the wealth of the Holy Office.

There is a story that the French troops made an extraordinary discovery when they entered the Palace of the Inquisition in Madrid. According to historian Eleanor Hibbert:

> One of the French officers, after having searched in vain for the dungeons of which he had heard, had the flagstones of the great hall taken up, and there below the floor discovered the cells and torture chambers. The French were reputed to have found victims still living among the dead. It was on this occasion that soldiers were said to have discovered that instrument of torture known as the Iron Virgin—a statue of the Virgin Mary the front of which was covered with sharp nails and daggers. The arms of this image could be moved to draw a victim close until the body of that victim was pierced by the nails and daggers.[57]

This finding merely served to increase the horror with which the Inquisition was viewed by the French and to justify their antagonism toward all that they saw as counterrevolutionary about the church.

When other European nations finally defeated Napoléon in 1813 and drove him from power, in many places old institutions, including the Inquisition, were brought back. In Spain, the restored monarch revived the Suprema in 1814. Revolutions swept across Spain six years later, and the Inquisition in Spain was again abolished in 1820.

Tribunal of Faith

Nevertheless, a body called the Tribunal of Faith made its appearance in 1823. Like the Suprema, it was designed to keep watch over the orthodoxy of the people in

The principles of the Inquisition had a long-lasting impact on the governments of Spain and Portugal, where heretics were sought out and punished into the middle of the nineteenth century.

Spain, but it operated differently. That the ideas of the Inquisition lingered was demonstrated by several unsuccessful efforts of the Spanish government to remove the inability to hold public office associated with "impure bloodlines."

Portugal, like Spain, continued to search for heretics into the middle of the nineteenth century. The liberal revolutions that swept across Spain also rocked Portugal in 1821 and temporarily drove out the Inquisition. The Holy Office made its reappearance, however, in 1852 in a set of religious codes every bit as intolerant as those that had been destroyed a few decades earlier. In Portugal as in Spain, the ideas of the Inquisition continued to influence the secular government in some form throughout the nineteenth century.

In Italy, lingering remnants of the Inquisition were destroyed by the armies of France. And while some elements of the Inquisition were restored after the defeat of Napoléon, these were very limited in their authority. After the defeat of the French, many Italians continued to see the Inquisition as an intrusion on their rights as Venetians, as citizens of Florence or Milan, and so on, just as they had for centuries.

Rome was a special case, since it was the seat of the papacy. The Inquisition was not abolished in Rome until 1852, when it was declared defunct as part of the movement to achieve Italian unification. The wealth of the Holy Office was taken over by the crown, the prisoners of the Roman Inquisition were released, and much of the archival material was burned, to the great irritation of later students of the history of the Inquisition in Rome.

In Latin America, the Spanish Inquisition continued its firm hold on the lives of people as long as Spain controlled its

Issued by Pope Leo X in 1559, the Papal Index was used by the church to control thought well into the twentieth century.

influences on the lives of many people in Latin America, were still in evidence late in the twentieth century.

In general, despite the survival of some local artifacts, it is clear that the French Revolution played an enormous role in destroying the physical institutions of the Inquisition. Prisons, archives, and implements of torture disappeared during the twenty-five years that French armies roamed Europe. Thus even during the reactionary period after the fall of Napoléon, it was not possible to reconstruct the Inquisition as it had existed.

The Papal Index

Nor was it possible to erase the ideas set forth by the French Revolution. Yet the church attempted to do just that. It wanted to turn back the clock to the time when it exercised control on popular thought through its control over literature. In this area, the Inquisition survived well into the twentieth century through a function known as the Papal Index—officially the Roman Index of Prohibited Books. Essentially a list of censored reading materials, the Papal Index was established in Rome in 1559. In that year Pope Leo X announced that

> [i]n all times to come no one should print, or cause to be printed, any book or other writing, either in Rome or any other city or diocese whatever, unless it were first approved, if in Rome, by the Pope's Vicar, and Master of the Sacred Palace; or, in other cities and dioceses, by the bishops, or some other person having understanding of science.

colonies. During the early part of the nineteenth century, the colonies gradually established their independence from Spain and as a result loosened the formal impact of the Inquisition on the lives of the people.

Yet, unlike their European counterparts, the people of Latin America continued to be dominated by powerful church-state cooperation. The ideas of the French Revolution, which had made deep inroads among the better-educated and more industrialized people of Europe, were less influential in the New World. As a result, remnants of the Inquisition, represented by conservative ecclesiastical

Books or writings proposed to be printed were to be diligently examined by the bishop or his delegate, and by the Inquisitor of Heretical Depravity, in the city or diocese where it was to be put to press, and approved by subscription under their own hand, to be given without fee, without delay, and under sentence of excommunication.[58]

Index Used to Control Thought

The purpose of the Index was to prevent dangerous books (particularly those written by Protestants or containing anticlerical themes) from reaching the public. The Inquisition in Rome, or the Holy Office, created a group of censors whose task it was to determine which writings fell into the dangerous category. These materials were placed on the Papal Index. In 1571 Pope Pius V created the Congregation of the Index, a separate agency to oversee the Index. Nonetheless, over the centuries, the Inquisition kept close watch over the publication of subversive reading materials.

Thousands of books have appeared on the Papal Index. The works of authors such as Erasmus, Savonarola, Machiavelli, and Boccaccio were banned. Parts of the works of other authors such as Dante were particularly censored, and some offending passages had to be removed before publication, although sometimes they were circulated privately. Scientific literature was particularly affected. Much of the work of such great men as Copernicus, Kepler, and Galileo was condemned by the church and banned for years from publication.

Erasmus is one of the many famous authors whose works were banned by the Papal Index for what the church considered "subversive" content.

Safe in England, the blind poet John Milton was able to ridicule the efforts of the Inquisition to control people's thoughts:

> To fill up the measure of that encroachment their last invention was to ordain that no book, pamphlet, or paper should be printed (as if St. Peter had bequeathed them the keys of the press also out of paradise) unless it were approved and licensed under the hands of two or three glutton friars.[59]

Control over ideas continued to be an extremely serious matter. Other Catholic countries, perhaps dissatisfied by the perceived leniency of the Papal Index, established their own lists of proscribed books. In Spain, for example, the list was much longer and the range of subjects much more far-reaching than that established in Rome.

The ban on the publication of certain books in Rome, Spain, and elsewhere had an interesting side effect. In places where the ban either did not exist or was not strictly enforced, the printing industry bloomed. Thus, while few books were published in Rome, from the middle of the sixteenth century onward in Venice, Switzerland, and elsewhere, a thriving industry provided books to an ever-increasing public.

England, where the Inquisition was never established, became the repository of an extensive collection of literature banned by the Inquisition during its first four hundred years. This came about because in the early seventeenth century, Thomas James, a scholar and contemporary of Milton, collected all the lists of proscribed books issued by the various indices in Europe. Then he recommended that the Bodleian Library at Oxford be sure to acquire at least one copy of each book on each list. A treasure thereby was preserved. Notes historian Edward Burman:

> If the Inquisition had been in a position to carry on throughout Europe, or even throughout the Catholic States, a censorship as effective as that put into force in Spain, the extermination of books would have been so considerable that there would have been brought about a serious break between the literatures of the centuries.[60]

While over time most aspects of the Inquisition gradually declined in importance or disappeared altogether, a new

official list of banned books was published by the Holy Office as recently as 1948. The Index itself was suspended, but not ended, in 1966.

Lessons of the Inquisition

The Inquisition tried to control the minds of millions of people for seven centuries, using what we today consider extreme forms of cruelty. Thousands, perhaps hundreds of thousands, of people fell into the clutches of the Holy Office. In the long

A revolutionary leader incites rebellion against the Inquisition. Despite seven centuries of torture, murder, and attempted thought control, the Inquisition ultimately failed to achieve uniformity of belief.

run, the Inquisition failed. Its vast network of offices and prisons and informers and inquisitors no longer exists.

In fact, the history of the Inquisition may even be seen as a source of hope because, as in the words of historian Bernard Hamilton, it demonstrates that

> [i]t is impossible to coerce belief. The Inquisition could, within limits, enforce outward conformity but it never succeeded in creating a united Christendom with a single belief—which was its goal. The history of that failure forms a valuable part of Western European experience.[61]

On the other hand, there may be less optimistic lessons to be drawn from the study of the Inquisition. Given the ability to exercise power over others, human beings have shown little restraint in their actions. The Inquisition was willing to tie to the stake and burn to death human beings who did not think and believe what those having power wished them to think and believe. In that context, the aphorism of the great nineteenth-century English Catholic philosopher Lord Acton may shed some light: "Power tends to corrupt and absolute power corrupts absolutely."

With that idea in mind, it may be that the history of the Inquisition is not an

A painting depicts Nero overseeing the persecution of Christians in ancient Rome. The Inquisition remains a grim reminder that throughout history humans have used cruel measures to impose their ideas on others.

An Inquisitorial Prison of Rome

In 1852 the historian William Harris Rule received a letter from a friend in the Italian army who had been present when an inquisitorial prison was opened to the public. In History of the Inquisition, *Rule cites a passage from that letter.*

"The condemned were immersed in a bath of slaked lime [a highly corrosive substance that would have eaten away the flesh of the victims], gradually filled up to their necks. The lime, by little and little, enclosed the sufferers, or walled them up all alive. The torment was extreme, but slow. As the lime rose higher and higher, the respiration of the victims became more and more painful, and because of the anguish of a compressed breathing, they died in a manner most horrible and desperate. Some time after their deaths, the heads would naturally separate from the bodies, and roll way into the hollows left by the lime."

aberration at all. It may be just another case of some people attempting to use brute force to impose their ideas on others. It may be yet another graphic example of the nature of human beings.

The Roman historian Tacitus left a dramatic account of the treatment accorded Christians by the emperor Nero following the Great Fire of Rome in A.D. 64:

> Dressed in wild animals' skins, they were torn to pieces by dogs, or crucified, or made into torches to be ignited after dark as substitutes for daylight. Nero provided his Gardens for the spectacle, and exhibited displays in the Circus [arena], at which he mingled with the crowd—or stood in a chariot dressed as a charioteer.[62]

Descendants of the very Christians who were lit and used as human torches dealt a thousand years later with those who questioned the church in the very same manner. And the performance of Nero is not that different from the work of the inquisitors-general who provided the crowds of Madrid with a fine auto-da-fé in the summer of 1680.

The twentieth century, rather than affording a respite in this dire account of man's inhumanity to man, may instead provide evidence to darken the outlook. We have only to think about Hitler, Stalin, and Franco, the killing fields of Cambodia, and the slaughter in Afghanistan, Bosnia, Somalia, Rwanda, and Burundi for examples of the intolerance of religious and ethnic diversity.

What separates us from our ancestors may simply be an increase in the technological efficiency with which we slaughter one another. Given the history of the Inquisition, it may be worthwhile to consider this awesome facet of human nature.

Notes

Chapter 1: The Establishment of the Inquisition

1. Carl Stephenson, *Mediaeval History.* New York: Harper & Brothers, 1951.

2. A. L. Maycock, *The Inquisition.* London: Constable, 1926.

3. Bernard Hamilton, *The Medieval Inquisition.* New York: Holmes & Meier, 1981.

4. Quoted in Hamilton, *The Medieval Inquisition.*

5. Fernand Hayward, *The Inquisition.* Paris: Librairie Arthème Fayard, 1965.

6. G. G. Coulton, *Inquisition and Liberty.* London: Heinemann, 1938.

7. Coulton, *Inquisition and Liberty.*

8. Coulton, *Inquisition and Liberty.*

9. Edward Burman, *The Inquisition: The Hammer of Heresy.* London: Aquarian Press, 1984.

Chapter 2: The Structure of the Inquisition

10. Hayward, *The Inquisition.*

11. Burman, *The Inquisition.*

12. Quoted in Burman, *The Inquisition.*

13. Quoted in Coulton, *Inquisition and Liberty.*

14. Quoted in Burman, *The Inquisition.*

15. Quoted in Burman, *The Inquisition.*

16. Quoted in Maycock, *The Inquisition.*

17. Henry Charles Lea, *A History of the Inquisition of Spain.* New York: Macmillan, 1906.

18. Quoted in William Harris Rule, *History of the Inquisition.* London: Wesleyan Conference Office, 1868.

19. Edward Peters, *Inquisition.* New York: Free Press, 1988.

20. Quoted in Coulton, *Inquisition and Liberty.*

21. Quoted in Burman, *The Inquisition.*

Chapter 3: The Spanish Inquisition

22. Quoted in John E. Longhurst, *The Age of Torquemada.* Lawrence, KS: Coronado Press, 1964.

23. Frederic David Mocatta, *The Jews of Spain and Portugal and the Inquisition.* 1933. Reprinted New York: Cooper Square Publishers, 1973.

24. Quoted in Paul J. Hauben, ed., *The Spanish Inquisition.* New York: Wiley, 1969.

25. Gustav Henningsen, ed., *The Inquisition in Early Modern Europe.* Dekalb: Northern Illinois University Press, 1986.

26. Quoted in Longhurst, *The Age of Torquemada.*

27. Quoted in Thomas Hope, *Torquemada, Scourge of the Jews.* London: Allen & Unwin, 1939.

28. Quoted in Longhurst, *The Age of Torquemada.*

Chapter 4: The Punishment of Sinners

29. Quoted in Coulton, *Inquisition and Liberty.*

30. Quoted in Maycock, *The Inquisition.*

31. Coulton, *Inquisition and Liberty.*

32. Quoted in Rule, *History of the Inquisition.*

33. Burman, *The Inquisition.*

34. Quoted in Maycock, *The Inquisition.*

35. Quoted in Maycock, *The Inquisition.*

36. Eleanor Hibbert, *The End of the Spanish Inquisition.* London: Robert Hale, 1961.

37. Rule, *History of the Inquisition.*

38. Rule, *History of the Inquisition.*

39. Coulton, *Inquisition and Liberty.*

Chapter 5: Famous Victims of the Inquisition

40. Jeffrey Burton Russell, *A History of Medieval Christianity.* New York: Crowell, 1968.

41. Quoted in Maycock, *The Inquisition*.

42. Quoted in Coulton, *Inquisition and Liberty*.

43. Quoted in Hibbert, *The End of the Spanish Inquisition*.

44. Quoted in Joseph R. Strayer, *The Middle Ages*. New York: Appleton-Century-Crofts, 1959.

45. Stephenson, *Mediaeval History*.

46. Hugh Trevor-Roper, "The European Witch Craze of the Sixteenth and Seventeenth Centuries," in M. Marwich, ed., *Witchcraft and Sorcery*. New York: Penguin, 1970.

47. Quoted in Stephenson, *Mediaeval History*.

48. Burman, *The Inquisition*.

49. Burman, *The Inquisition*.

50. Quoted in Sir Alexander Cardew, *A Short History of the Inquisition*. London: Watts, 1933.

51. Quoted in Matthew Spinka, *Jan Hus and the Council of Constance*. New York: Columbia University Press, 1965.

52. Barbara Tuchman, *The March of Folly: From Troy to Vietnam*. New York: Knopf, 1984.

53. Quoted in Burman, *The Inquisition*.

54. Quoted in Hayward, *The Inquisition*.

55. Hayward, *The Inquisition*.

56. Quoted in Rule, *History of the Inquisition*.

Chapter 6: The Gradual End of the Inquisition

57. Hibbert, *The End of the Spanish Inquisition*.

58. Quoted in Burman, *The Inquisition*.

59. Quoted in Burman, *The Inquisition*.

60. Burman, *The Inquisition*.

61. Hamilton, *The Medieval Inquisition*.

62. Quoted in Tacitus Cornelius, *The Works of Tacitus*. New York: Harper, 1889-91.

Glossary

auto-da-fé: Portuguese term for "act of faith": the public ceremony during which people found guilty by the Inquisition were informed of their punishments. Executions were carried out promptly by the civil authorities.

"Babylonian captivity": Period from 1314 through 1378 when the popes resided in Avignon, France, and were under the control of the French kings.

coroza: The high pointed hat of shame worn by people who were being publicly punished by the Spanish Inquisition.

Council of Trent: Church authorities who met intermittently from 1545 until 1563, condemned the Reformation, and defined church doctrine, including the establishment of the Papal Index, the list of books Roman Catholics were forbidden to read.

Dominicans: Order of monks founded by Domingo de Guzman (1170-1221). The Dominicans were very frequently selected as inquisitors because their rigorous education enabled them to question suspected heretics in a thorough manner.

edict of faith: The proclamation by an inquisitor of the commencement in a given locality of an investigation into the purity of the beliefs of his listeners.

executioner's rods: The staffs used by agents of the Inquisition to beat persons being punished.

familiars: Agents of the inquisitorial courts, frequently spies, who attempted to identify people in a district against whom the Holy Office might take judicial action.

Fraticelli: Franciscan monks who insisted on living in poverty, in emulation of the early Christians and the founder of their order, Francis of Assisi.

garroting: Strangulation.

Great Schism: Period from 1378 until 1409 when the Catholic Church had two popes.

Innocent III: The pope who launched the Albigensian crusade against the Cathars.

limpieze de sangre: "Purity of blood"; at one time a precondition to holding public office in Spain.

murus largus: Punishment of imprisonment that could be served in a hospital or convent, assisting in good works.

murus stricturus: Punishment of imprisonment for life.

Papal Index: List of books Roman Catholics were forbidden to read without special permission.

period of grace: Period of approximately thirty days between the proclamation of an edict of faith and the date the Inquisition began rounding up suspects.

relapsed sinner: A person who has maintained unorthodox religious views, repented, and then returns to his or her heretical ways; also, a person who converts to Christianity, perhaps under pressure, and returns to his or her original faith.

sanbenitos: The yellow sleeveless robes worn by penitents in autos-da-fé and by persons whose punishment from the Inquisition included public humiliation.

Tomás de Torquemada: Spanish Dominican monk who convinced King Ferdinand and Queen Isabella to drive the Jews of Spain from their homeland; served as his country's inquisitor-general and was the architect of the Spanish Inquisition.

Peter Waldo: Founder of the Waldensians, also known as the Poor Men of Lyons, fundamentalist Christian laymen who incurred the wrath of the Inquisition.

For Further Reading

Sir Alexander Cardew, *A Short History of the Inquisition*. London: Watts, 1933. Provides information illustrating the complex motives of people who were in charge of the Inquisition.

Thomas Hope, *Torquemada, Scourge of the Jews*. London: Allen & Unwin, 1939. Biography of the monk who shaped the Spanish Inquisition. Offers insights into the mind of the man who wanted to establish racial purity in Spain.

Henry Charles Lea, *A History of the Inquisition of Spain*. New York: Macmillan, 1906. This three-volume work on the Inquisition paved the way for many of the major studies in the twentieth century. An exhaustive source of information on all aspects of the Inquisition.

Mary Elizabeth Perry and Anne J. Cruz, *Cultural Encounters: The Impact of the Inquisition in Spain in the New World*. Berkeley: University of California Press, 1991. A very useful book describing the interrelations between the structures of the Spanish Inquisition and the unique characteristics of the Inquisition as it developed in the New World.

Cecil Roth, *A History of the Marranos*. Philadelphia: Jewish Publication Society of America, 1932. This very insightful but partisan account was written by an eminent English historian. The book describes the lives of the secret Jews of Spain.

Rafael Sabatini, *Torquemada and the Spanish Inquisition*. London: Stanley Paul, 1913. Contains enormous detail regarding the life and times of the man who helped guide the development of the Inquisition in Spain.

Matthew Spinka, *Jan Hus and the Council of Constance*. New York: Columbia University Press, 1965. Scholarly work dealing with the complexities of the controversy between Jan Hus and the dominant influences of the church in Europe.

Carl Stephenson, *Mediaeval History*. New York: Harper & Brothers, 1951. An extremely learned text that provides a broad range of information. Most useful in terms of understanding the Inquisition in the context of the Middle Ages.

Hugh Trevor-Roper, "The European Witch Craze of the Sixteenth and Seventeenth Centuries," in M. Marwich, ed., *Witchcraft and Sorcery*. New York: Penguin, 1970. Offers insights into the relation between witchcraft and heresy as seen by the Inquisition.

Additional Works Consulted

Roland H. Bainton, *The Medieval Church*. Princeton, NJ: D. Van Nostrand Company, Inc., 1962.

Edward Burman, *The Inquisition: The Hammer of Heresy*. London: Aquarian Press, 1984. Short but very informative book that provides a broad picture of the Inquisition from its development as an instrument to destroy the Cathars in the thirteenth century through its survival into the twentieth century.

Tacitus Cornelius, *The Works of Tacitus*. New York: Harper, 1889-91. This is a well-designed and useful edition of the works of Tacitus.

G. G. Coulton, *Inquisition and Liberty*. London: Heinemann, 1938. A description of the Inquisition by a historian who has a strong anti-Catholic bias. The book is extremely useful in providing information regarding the excesses of the Inquisition.

John Gage, *Life in Italy at the Time of the Medici*. New York: Capricorn Books, 1968. A colorful depiction of the turmoil caused by Savonarola.

Stephen Haliczer, ed., *Inquisition and Society in Early Modern Europe*. Totowa, NJ: Barnes and Noble, 1987. Series of articles dealing with the Inquisition in Spain and Spanish-controlled lands. Interesting material on the numbers of people tried by the Inquisition and the amounts of money involved in court cases.

Bernard Hamilton, *The Medieval Inquisition*. New York: Holmes & Meier, 1981. An excellent short summary of the history of the medieval Inquisition through the end of the fourteenth century.

Paul J. Hauben, ed., *The Spanish Inquisition*. New York: Wiley, 1969. Collection of documents relating to various aspects of the Spanish Inquisition; provides provocative information regarding different interpretations of the Inquisition.

Fernand Hayward, *The Inquisition*. Paris: Librairie Arthème Fayard, 1965. A concise history of the Inquisition that traces the development of the institution from its roots in the elimination of the Cathars to its development in Spain in the fifteenth century. A strong defense of the actions taken by the Catholic Church through the Inquisition.

Gustav Henningsen, ed., *The Inquisition in Early Modern Europe*. Dekalb: Northern Illinois University Press, 1986. Contains a collection of essays dealing with a study of the archives of the Inquisition in Spain, Italy, and elsewhere. The book explains how inquisitorial records can be used to study the social and psychological as well as religious mind-sets of the people who directed the various national inquisitions.

Eleanor Hibbert, *The End of the Spanish Inquisition*. London: Robert Hale, 1961. Strong condemnation of the Spanish Inquisition. The case records provided illustrate the role played by financial considerations in the selection of victims.

Henry Kamen, *The Spanish Inquisition.* New York: New American Library, 1965. This Marxist interpretation of the Inquisition offers an interesting discussion of the class struggle between the bourgeois Jews and laboring Moors against aristocratic Spanish Catholic landowning classes.

Seymour B. Liebman, *The Inquisitors and the Jews in the New World.* Miami, FL: University of Miami Press, 1974. Collection of excerpts from the transactions of the Inquisition in the New World. This is a useful review of the history of many of the New Christians in the New World and demonstrates how they were caught up in the courts of the Inquisition.

John E. Longhurst, *The Age of Torquemada.* Lawrence, KS: Coronado Press, 1964. This fiery statement of the case against the Spanish church attacks the anti-Semitic, racist policies of the Spanish church, the Spanish government, and the Catholic hierarchy in their dealings with the Jewish and converted Jewish communities of Spain in the fourteenth and fifteenth centuries.

A. L. Maycock, *The Inquisition.* London: Constable, 1926. Interesting account written by a Catholic historian. Attempts to explain the history of the Inquisition in terms of the expectations of the people who lived in fifteenth-century Spain.

Frederic David Mocatta, *The Jews of Spain and Portugal and the Inquisition.* 1933. Reprinted New York: Cooper Square Publishers, 1973. Short account, filled with interesting details of the Inquisition from the perspective of the Jews of Spain.

Edward Peters, *Inquisition.* New York: Free Press, 1988. Very interesting perspective on the relationship of religion to the state. The historian presents a picture of the Inquisition in the context of the Roman Catholic tradition of controlling heresy as a threat to society.

————, ed., *Heresy and Authority in Medieval Europe.* Philadelphia: University of Pennsylvania Press, 1988. A very useful collection of texts dealing with aspects of European heresy from late antiquity to the period of early English reformer John Wycliffe.

William Harris Rule, *History of the Inquisition.* London: Wesleyan Conference Office, 1868. An excellent source of information from a Briton who experienced some effects of the Inquisition. This Protestant clergyman's account offers unusual insights into the workings of the Inquisition in the nineteenth century.

Jeffrey Burton Russell, *A History of Medieval Christianity.* New York: Crowell, 1968. A short, concise, very readable account of developments in the medieval church.

Joseph R. Strayer, *The Middle Ages.* New York: Appleton-Century-Crofts, 1959. A well-written history of the Middle Ages from the perspective of an English Protestant.

Barbara Tuchman, *The March of Folly: From Troy to Vietnam.* New York: Knopf, 1984. Attempts to provide new and unusual insights into the Middle Ages.

Index

Picture Credits

Cover photo by the Bettmann Archive

Alinari/Art Resource, NY, 25, 93, 99, 111

The Ancient Art & Architecture Collection, 11, 14, 17, 29, 31, 47, 54, 65, 66, 73, 76, 78

The Bettmann Archive, 13, 16, 19, 21, 23, 24, 30, 39 (both), 40, 41, 44, 45, 49, 50, 53, 56, 58, 61, 62, 67, 68, 71 (both), 77, 81, 83, 84, 86, 92, 95, 98, 100, 102, 106, 110, 112

Bridgeman Art Library/Art Resource, NY, 10, 36, 108

Giraudon/Art Resource, NY, 85 (top), 105

© Erich Lessing/Art Resource, NY, 75, 87

Library of Congress, 59, 89, 91 (top), 101

North Wind Picture Archives, 104, 107, 109

Scala/Art Resource, NY, 22

Stock Montage, Inc., 20, 26, 28, 33, 34, 38, 43, 51, 70, 74, 82, 85 (bottom), 90, 91 (bottom), 97

About the Author

Deborah Bachrach was born and raised in New York City, where she received her undergraduate education. She earned a Ph.D. in history from the University of Minnesota. Dr. Bachrach has taught at the University of Minnesota as well as at St. Francis College, Joliet, Illinois, and Queens College, the City University of New York. In addition, she has worked for many years in the fields of medical research and public policy development.